ॐ Saraswatyanamah

Bhagawad Gita
and
Ananya Bhakti

Gorti Visweswara Rao

Dedication

BHAGAVAD GITA is truly a song by Bhagawaan rather than a message. It reverberates in our minds even with a single reading. I dedicate this small volume to my (late) parents Manikyamba and Suryanarayana who bestowed on me this body, mind and intellect so that I am able to conveniently and fully offer prayers to God Almighty and remember HIM constantly.

Contents

Little Sri Krishna - Bhavayami Gopala balam

Before proceeding forward, I wish to remind myself and you all about the devotional song *"Bhavayami Gopala balam"*, written by Tallapaka Annamacharya[1] (1408-1503) and also known as Annamaya. Through this delightful song, I like to recollect those divine playful actions of little Sri Krishna playing in Gokula and entertaining HIS[2] mother Yashoda and also all the divine gods Brahma and the heavenly deities.

---

1   Tallapaka Annamacharya belongs to a region called Tallapaka, Near Tirupati, in Andhra Pradesh. He is a devout worshipper of *Paramaatma* and he is a well-known composer of many *kirtanas* / songs as well as a singer. His *kirtanas* written in Telugu language are in praise of Lord Venkateswara of Tirumala or popularly known as TTD in Andhra Pradesh. The musical_form of the *kirtana* songs that he composed, are hugely popular with Carnatic_music concerts.

2   The pronouns HE, HIM, HIS and HIMSELF in capital letters used in the text, stand for *Paramaatma,* the supreme GOD Almighty.

భావయామి గోపాలబాలం
మన-స్సేవితం తత్పదం చింతయేహం
సదా ||

కటి ఘటిత మేఖలా ఖచితమణి ఘంటికా-
పటల నినదేన విభ్రాజమానమ్ |
కుటిల పద ఘటిత సంకుల శింజితేన తం
చటుల నటనా సముజ్జ్వల విలాసమ్ ||
నిరతకర కలిత నవనీతం బ్రహ్మది
సుర నికర భావనా శోభిత పదమ్ |
తిరువేంకటాచల స్థితమ్ అనుపమం హరిం
పరమ పురుషం గోపాలబాలమ్ ||

Annamaya

The song carries us away into the beautiful sparkling Divine world of Gokula. In the song, Annamacharya (also known as Annamaya) describes Little Krishna: how HE is radiant and charming and looking resplendent, *i.e.,* glittering due to the tinkling of his ornaments on HIS waist and wrists. Even with his uneven and curved steps (because of being a small child), his unsteady walk resembles a graceful dance. The song is a lovely depiction of *Paramatma*'s *leela* or *Paramaatma*'s mesmerizing divine actions that had been visualized by Annamaya and wonderfully projected before our eyes to our fortune. This is indeed '*maanasica puja*', i.e., worship of *Paramaatma* by mind. Annamaya had provided that spiritual chance to us also, to participate in the *maanasica puja*.

Author's Self-Introduction

Before I proceed to the introductory part of the book, I need to make the author's introduction. So, I need to make self-introduction. Introducing oneself by self may seem to be incongruous or inappropriate and particularly more so in the context of my bold attempt in writing a few words about Bhagavad Gita and when the very message in Gita is about discarding all self-possessions including the annexures like 'mine', 'myself', 'I am' and such self-identities. Thus, I got engulfed by such initial momentary state of deluded mind. But, I need to come out of this misperception. Treating this requirement of penning my own introduction as Bhagawaan[3]'s directive, I write the following few words about myself:

Place of birth: Amalapuram in East Godavari district, Andhra Pradesh, India.

Date of birth: 20th Aug. 1947 and I already entered into my 78th year in this mortal world.

Education: BSc.: 1965. SKBR College, Amalapuram, East Godavari district, Andhra Pradesh, India.

BE: 1968. Government College of Engineering, Kakinada, East Godavari district, Andhra Pradesh, India

PhD: 1989. Indian Institute of Science, Bangalore, India

Books: Coauthored a couple of engineering books with a Professor friend in Indian Institute of Science, Bangalore

---

3   The words *Bhagawaan, Paramaatma,* Supreme Soul, Infinite Soul and *Purushothama* are used as synonyms.

Present interests: Trying to engage myself in *Paramaatma*'s thoughts wherever and whenever it is possible and about HIS this grand and mysterious *srusthi i.e.,* creation of this beautiful world and the mysteries surrounding our mortal lives.

Also my engagements include giving guest lectures on my engineering subject, of course, with constant remembrance in mind of the following *sloka[4] (hymn) in the superb composition of Bhaja Govindam* written in Sanskrit – by Adi Sankaracharya[5].

Let us first have the context of the *sloka* in '*Bhajagovindam*'. Addressing an elderly person who is found struggling to learn Sanskrit grammar, Adi Sankaracharya says in the hymn implying a rebuke, 'Oh ignorant soul! worship Govinda, worship Govinda. Rules of grammar won't save you at the time of your death'; Here note that Govinda is another name to Sri Krishna, the incarnate of *Paramaatma in Dwapur yuga.*

---

4   Words of Sanskrit are mostly written in italicized words in the book

5   Adi Sankaracharya of 8th century was born in a place called Kaladi in Kerala state, India. He renounced the world at an early age in quest of Truth and was initiated into hermitic life by the great ascetic Govindapada. Before his death at an early age of thirty-two, Sankaracharya travelled the length and breadth of India preaching the divinity of soul and established the omnipotence of non-dualistic Vedanta. *Bhaja govindam* is classified as a *prakarana grantha*, a primer to the major works of Adi Sankaracharya. It contains the whole essence of *Vedanta* and true purpose of this mortal life.

भज गोविन्दं भज गोविन्दं
गोविन्दं भज मूढमते ।
सम्प्राप्ते सन्निहिते काले
नहि नहि रक्षति डुकृङ्करणे

Bhajagovindam

<u>Meaning:</u>

Worship Govinda,

worship Govinda,

worship Govinda, Oh fool!

Rules of grammar will not save you at

the time of your death.

Adi Sankaracharya

Adi Sankaracharya in this *sloka* advises an ignorant old man and obviously all ignorant souls like me to worship Govinda, the God Almighty, the Supreme *Parama Purusha*. He further advises that rules of grammar won't help anyone at the time of his death. In other words, he asks us to stop all actions that are usually performed by all of us with all sorts of desires and which will not help in understanding the reality of this mortal life.

This *sloka* always comes to my mind and strikes my face whenever I feel bloated up or feel proud of "oh! I achieved something or I became successful in this task". But is it true that it is all due to the so-called my own effort only? That feeling is misplaced and absolutely wrong. Hope, I made it clear why I remember this *sloka* always. If one can achieve whatever she / he embarks upon, the basic tenet of this mortal life is lost in the sense that we may not be able to imagine a world with no differences either in intelligence or prosperity or by any other yardstick.

If I now proceed forward, let me now delve into a short prelude or introduction which I treat it as *"my humble mind's musings or my humble mind's thoughts"*.

Slokas from Bhagavad Gita Referred to in the Order of their Presence in the Book

The prelude	*sloka*	number in Bhagavad Gita	name of the chapter
	चतुर्विधा भजन्ते मां	16	*Jnaana Vijnaana yoga*
	तेषां ज्ञानी नित्ययुक्त	17	
	अभ्यासयोगयुक्तेन	8	*Akshara Para Brahma Yoga*
	गतिर्भर्ता प्रभुः साक्षी	18	*Rajavidya Rajaguhya yoga*
	तेषामेवानुकम्पार्थम	11	*Vibhuti yoga*
	उद्धरेदात्मनात्मानं	5	*Aatmasanyama yoga*
	बन्धुरात्मात्मनस्तस्य	6	
	महात्मानस्तु मां	13	*Rajavidya Rajaguhya yoga*
	सततं कीर्तयन्तो मां	14	
	पत्रं पुष्पं फलं तोयं	26	

Chapter 1	*sloka*	number in Bhagavad Gita	name of the chapter
	देवद्विजगुरुप्राज्ञपूजनं	14	*Sradhatriya vibhaga yoga*
	अनुद्वेगकरं वाक्यं	15	
	मनः प्रसादः सौम्यत्वं	16	
	श्रद्धया परया तप्तं	17	
	असंशयं महाबाहो	35	*Aatmasanyama yoga*
	यदा हि नेन्द्रियार्थेषु	4	
	मय्यावेश्य मनो ये	2	*Bhakti yoga*
	ज्ञानयज्ञेन चाप्यन्ये	15	*Rajavidya Rajaguhya yoga*
	यो यो यां यां तनुं	21	*Jnaana Vijnaana yoga*
	अथ चित्तं समाधातुं न	9	*Bhakti yoga*
	अभ्यासेऽप्यसमर्थोऽसि	10	
	अथैतदप्यशक्तोऽसि	11	
	समोऽहं सर्वभूतेषु	29	*Rajavidya Rajaguhya yoga*
	अविभक्तं च भूतेषु	16	*Kshetra Kshetrajna yoga*
	यद्यद्विभूतिमत्सत्त्वं	41	*Vibhuti yoga*
	ये तु सर्वाणि कर्माणि	6	*Bhakti yoga*
	तेषामहं समुद्धर्ता	7	
	चतुर्विधा भजन्ते मां	16	*Jnaana Vijnaana yoga*

Chapter 2	*sloka*	number in Bhagavad Gita	name of the chapter
	मच्चित्ता मद्गतप्राणा	9	*Vibhuti yoga*
	अपि चेत्सुदुराचारो	30	*Rajavidya Rajaguhya yoga*
	इच्छाद्वेषसमुत्थेन	27	*Jnaana Vijnaana yoga*
	येषां त्वन्तगतं पापं	28	
	चेतसा सर्वकर्माणि	57	*Mokshasanyasa yoga*

Chapter 3	*sloka*	number in Bhagavad Gita	name of the chapter
	उपद्रष्टानुमन्ता च	22	*Kshetra Kshetrajna Yoga*

Chapter 4	*sloka*	number in Bhagavad Gita	name of the chapter
	बाह्यस्पर्शेष्वसक्तात्मा	21	*Karmasanyasa yoga*
	प्रशान्तमनसं होनं	27	*Aatmasayama yoga*
	मां च योऽव्यभिचारेण	26	*Gunatriyavibhaga yoga*
	सर्वकर्माण्यपि सदा	56	*Mokshasanyasa yoga*

The epilogue	*sloka*	number in Bhagavad Gita	name of the chapter
	त्रिविधं नरकस्येदं	21	*Daivaasura Sampad Vibhhaaga Yoga*
	बुद्ध्या विशुद्धया युक्तो	51	*Mokshasanyasa Yoga*
	विविक्तसेवी लघ्वाशी	52	
	अहङ्कारं बलं दर्प	53	

The Prelude -
A Humble Mind's Musings

It is true that when I was struck with an idea of producing this Book and simultaneously pen my thoughts in praise of *Paramaatma*, the creator of this beautiful world, my enthusiasm knew no bounds and was beyond any words to speak about. But, surprisingly, even to make a little start, I felt drained of all my mental faculties initially and had to struggle hard to gather my wits again, come to terms with myself and complete the task - undoubtedly with HIS blessings alone.

What is this book about? and *what is the objective?*

In this book, my prime idea is to focus completely and converge fully on to the sublime theme of *Ananya bhakti* (unbounded or unflinching exclusive devotion) that one needs to develop towards *Paramaatma*. As readers may be already familiar with the divine teachings of Bhagawaan Sri Krishna in Bhagavad Gita, we find almost in all *slokas* (hymns) - to our astonishment on one hand and to our enlightenment on the other – the persistent and untiring message from the *Viswa Guru* about HIS love and affection towards a true devotee. This message is the driving force in writing this book. In this context, I remind myself and of course all of you also, of the following two *slokas* in *Jnana Vijnana yoga* of Bhagavad Gita:

1st *sloka*

चतुर्विधा भजन्ते मां जनाः सुकृतिनोऽर्जुन ।
आर्ती जिज्ञासुरर्थार्थी ज्ञानी च भरतर्षभ ॥ १६ ॥

2nd *sloka*

तेषां ज्ञानी नित्ययुक्त एकभक्तिर्विशिष्यते ।
प्रियो हि ज्ञानिनोऽत्यर्थमहं स च मम प्रियः ॥ १७॥

Jnana Vijnana yoga

Meaning: Bhagawaan says in these *slokas*: Virtuous persons worship HIM; HE describes them to be of four types. i) those persons in distress, ii) seekers of knowledge, iii) seekers of enjoyment and iv) those endowed with wisdom. Of these *bhaktaas* (devotees), the *jnani* (wise man) with a single minded devotion, surrenders himself to HIM. Such a devotee is dear to HIM and in turn HE is dear to the devotee.

Total surrender and Ananya bhakti

So, it is total surrender and *ananya bhakti* that bring us close and dearer to *Paramaatma*. When one is blessed with this strong conviction, what more nourishment is required! But, immediately, as usual, because of our mere mortal weakness and because of a doubt on our own capabilities: what we think? The total surrender and getting close to *Paramaatma* - Is this possible? Is it an easily acquirable quality by us?

To clear our doubt or this misconception, we need to pause for a moment and rewind in our minds what all message we received from Bhagawaan Sri Krishna in Bhagavad Gita. Also, we need to accept that, in a class, all may not belong to the top few brilliant students. There may be much less than 1 to 2 percent only who may be the blessed few who grasp everything quickly. Not only assimilating, but also they become practical and successful. In our context, Sri Ramakrishna Paramahamsa,

Sri Raman Maharshi, Swami Vivekananda - these luminaries are such accomplished *jnanis* who had gone close and become dear to *Paramaatma*.

But, even ordinary students like me also definitely can make a try to elevate ourselves. By sheer determination, and by recapitulating, *i.e.,* making a recap, *i.e.,* by going through Bhagawaan's message again and again, we will definitely find the solution. What is it ?

It is true dedication, control of all our senses and nurturing deep and unwavering devotion towards *Paramaatma* that bless any determined person with the dearest spot nearest to *Paramaatma*.

This is indeed the true essence of Bhagavad Gita.

In this context, let us recall the message by Bhagawaan Sri Krishna in *Akshara Para Brahma Yoga*:

अभ्यासयोगयुक्तेन चेतसा नान्यगामिना ।

परमं पुरुषं दिव्यं याति पार्थानुचिन्तयन् ॥ ८ ॥

Akshara Para Brahma Yoga

Meaning: Whoever gets engaged in the constant practice of not allowing the mind to wander away to anything else and whoever meditates solely on the supreme *Paramaatma*, reaches HIM

So, this is the vital truth which one needs to drive hard into one's mind without any shadow of doubt.

Here, I also remember the final prayers by Gajendra, the immortal devotee in *Gajendra Moksham* – which is one of the most illustrative episodes in *Srimad Bhagavatam*

Veda Vyasa

written by Veda Vyasa[6] in Sanskrit. It demonstrates the power of *ananya bhakti* and total surrender on the part of true devotee. Bammera Pothana[7] (1450–1510) is well-known for his scholarly translation of *Srimad Bhagavatam* into Telugu language by name *Sri Maha Bhagavatamu.*

Pothana

What I now wish to recount is the poem in Gajendra Moksham from this translation *Sri MahaBhagavatamu* by Pothana.

The context in the poem is as follows:

Gajendra, the elephant is battling for life in a fight with a crocodile. It gets into a state of helplessness and desperation and looks up for help from the God almighty. Through the elephant's desperate prayer to *Paramaatma*, the saintly poet Pothana shows his depth of *ananya bhakti* and devotional fervour in describing *Paramaatma* in the poem, as the Iswara, *i.e.,* as the supreme creator and protector of this universe.

---

6   Vyasa is the legendary author of the *Srimad Bhagavata, Mahabharata, Vedas* and *Puranas* which are some of the most important works connected with the highest form of pure and transcendental philosophy of life. He is considered as the manifestation of Lord Vishnu, the God Almighty. He has compiled the single, eternal Veda into four separate parts —Rigveda, Samaveda, Yajurveda and Atharvaveda and hence he is commonly known as "Veda Vyasa". Bhagavad Gita is an episode present in *Mahabharata* and occupies chapters 23 to 40 of *Parva* (Section) 6 of *Mahabharata* in the form of a dialogue between the *Pandava* prince Arjuna and Sri Krishna.

7   Pothana is a saintly poet born in Bammera village, Telangana state, India and known for his astounding devotion towards Lord Rama (God incarnate in *Treta yuga*). He was a scholar in Telugu as well as Sanskrit. As a young man, he was known to be a devotee of Lord Siva. Later, realizing the Omnipresence of *Paramaatma* and the truth that all is ONE and that there is no difference between Siva and Vishnu, he became more interested in salvation and self-realization. He was of strong opinion that poetic compositions are a divine blessing and should be utilized for salvation by devoting them to the God Almighty.

ఎవ్వనిచే జనించు జగ; మెవ్వని లోపల నుండు లీనమై;
యెవ్వని యందు డిందు; బరమేశ్వరు డెవ్వడు; మూలకారణం
బెవ్వ; డనాదిమధ్యలయుడ డెవ్వడు; సర్వముదానయైన వాడ
డెవ్వడు; వాని నాత్మభవు నీశ్వరు నే శరణంబు వేడెదన్.

Gajendra moksham in MahaBhagavatamu by Pothana

Meaning: By_whom this whole world is created, in whom this whole world exists, within whom all this existence gets finally extinguished and merged, who is the supreme *Paramaatma,* who is the reason and the seed behind this *srushti* or creation, who has no beginning and end and who is eternal, to HIM I humbly appeal for shelter and help.

Here, if we pause and ponder over what we have heard from Sri Bhagawaan Sri Krishna on many occasions in Bhagawad Gita about the All–pervading, Omniscient, *i.e.,* All-knowing and boundless God Almighty, the following *sloka* in *Rajavidya Rajaguhya yoga* must come to our mind:

गतिर्भर्ता प्रभुः साक्षी निवासः शरणं सुहृत् ।
प्रभवः प्रलयः स्थानं निधानं बीजमव्ययम् ॥ १८ ॥

Rajavidya Rajaguhya yoga

Meaning: *Paramaatma* is the Goal, the Supporter, the Lord, the witness for everything, the destination for everyone, the Supreme shelter, the Friend, the in-dweller in all, the sustainer, destroyer, the foundation, the treasure-house and the seed which is imperishable.

If we refer back to Gajendra Moksham, Pothana in the following poem, describes how Gajendra, after all his strength got drained out in the battle for his life, how he totally surrendered and made an earnest and pitiable final appeal seeking for *Paramaatma*'s help: It is such a picturesque and vivid description that it is an extraordinary portrayal or exposition of Pothana's poetic excellence and his devotional fervor. The poem reads as:

లావొక్కింతయు లేదు ధైర్యము విలోలంబయ్యె ప్రాణంబులున్
రావుల్ దప్పెను మూర్ఛవచ్చె తనువున్ డస్సెన్ శ్రమం
బయ్యెడిన్
నీవే తప్ప నితఃపరం బెఱుగ మన్నింపం దగున్ దీనునిన్
రావే ఈశ్వర! కావవే వరద! సంరక్షింపు భద్రాత్మకా!

Gajendra moksham in MahaBhagavatamu by Pothana

I feel happy to give the meaning of this poem word by word, because the poet Pothana used very simple, unassuming words of day-to-day usage in Telugu language to convey such an extraordinary devotional appeal to *Paramaatma*. We cannot but feel an admiration for his poetic excellence.

లావొక్కింతయు లేదు - O Bhagawaan! I lost my strength

ధైర్యము విలోలంబయ్యె i.e., I have no more courage to fight

ప్రాణంబులున్ రావుల్ దప్పెను - I have reached my last moment.

మూర్ఛవచ్చె - I am losing my consciousness,

తనువున్ డస్సెన్ - My body got exhausted శ్రమం బయ్యెడిన్ - I am tired

నీవే తప్ప నితఃపరం బెఱుగ - I know YOU only and nobody else.

మన్నింపం దగున్ దీనునిన్ - I am in a miserable state and may be excused.

రావే ఈశ్వర - O Iswara, Ruler of this world! Please come.

కావవే వరద! - O Giver of boons! Please save me.

సంరక్షింపు భద్రాత్మకా - Protect me, O Noble Lord, and take me into your shelter.

What a wonderful and magnificent poem, it is !

This type of desperation, as you know, is common for all of us in moments of extreme distress. In fact, from this anecdote in *MahaBhagavatam*, Veda Vyasa and Pothana wish to convey to us all, a more deeper message with a sublime meaning. Apart from the seemingly simple expression in the poem, through the devotee's prayer the poets bring out and speak of the truth of this mortal life - about all its troubles and tribulations and the need for us to perpetually, *i.e.,* always to remain ourselves devoted to *Paramaatma*. The whole episode in Gajendra Moksham is reminiscent or indicative of a fervent and passionate appeal and submission from a devotee to the God Almighty, to grant him freedom from all shackles, *i.e.,* bondages from this mundane life and union with *Paramaatma*.

The message is clear: *It is ananya bhakti and total surrender to Paramaatma that lead a person to a higher state of self-learning.*

Here, it is very befitting to remind ourselves again about Bhagawaan's assurance in the following *sloka* in *Vibhuti yoga*:

तेषामेवानुकम्पार्थमहमज्ञानजं तमः ।
नाशयाम्यात्मभावस्थो ज्ञानदीपेन भास्वता ॥ ११ ॥

Vibhuti Yoga

Meaning: *Paramaatma* is the in-dweller in every heart and soul. To the devotees who have totally dedicated themselves to *Paramaatma*, HE shines the lamp of knowledge in them and extinguishes or removes from their minds the darkness born out of ignorance.

How much benevolent *Paramaatma* is! That lamp of knowledge from *Paramaatma*, we need to aspire for in this mortal life. And for that, we need to endeavor and make right effort to deserve HIS benevolence. Towards creating this awareness only in commoners like me, the great personalities in the ancient past and our present times also strived hard to inculcate a spirit of introspection or realization of the self within and to make us awakened so as to recognize the true values of this short and impermanent life.

Here, we need to place our utmost attention to what *Sri Adi Sankaracharya* advised in *Saadhana Panchakam*[8]. It is quite illuminating and contains steps to uplift our level of thinking and to properly channelize our activities. The specific advice given in the last verse of the composition reads as:

एकान्ते सुखमास्यतां परतरे चेतः समाधीयतां
पूर्णात्मा सुसमीक्ष्यतां जगदिदं तद्बाधितं
दृश्यताम्।
प्राक्कर्म प्रविलाप्यतां चितिबलान्नाप्युत्तरैः
श्लिष्यतां
प्रारब्धं त्विह भुज्यतामथ परब्रह्मात्मना
स्थीयताम् ॥ ॥५॥

Saadhana Panchakam

Adi Sankaracharya

> **Meaning:** In solitude, live joyously, quieten your mind in the Supreme *Paramaatma*, realise and see the All-pervading Self everywhere. Recognise that the finite universe is a projection of the Supreme Self. Eradicate *prarabha karma* by the present right action, *i.e.,* conquer the effects of the deeds done in earlier lives by the present right action. Through wisdom, become detached from future actions. Thereafter, live absorbed in the thought – "I am Brahman! "

One will be overwhelmingly amazed by the teachings of all these great personalities. Sri Ramana Maharshi[9] always insisted on self-enquiry

Sri Ramana Maharshi

— enquiry into one's own self. From one of his most illuminating writings by name "Who Am I? (Nan Yar?

The Teachings of Bhagavaan Sri Ramana Maharshi",

I quote here what he has said on self-enquiry.

He has said:

"Enquiry consists in retaining the mind in the Self. Meditation consists in thinking that one's self is Brahman, the existence-consciousness-bliss".

This message carries the simplest but the most valuable advice for all of us.

---

9   *Sri Ramana Maharshi* [1879-1950]– One of the greatest spiritual sages; Revered for his teaching of self-inquiry in the form of the divine message *'know thyself '*; Worshipped by all for his direct teaching through silence

We also find Sri Ramakrishna Paramahamsa[10] giving us the magical advice:

"utter the word Gita, in quick succession, a number of times – *gita – gita – gita*. It is then virtually pronounced as '*tagi – tagi – tagi*'.

Sri Ramakrishna Paramahamsa

This word '*tagi*' means one who has renounced the world for the sake of God. Thus, in one word, Sri Ramakrishna Paramahamsa (Sri Sri Ramakrishna Kathamrita –III) has said the whole truth the Gita contains:

"Renounce, ye world-bound men! Renounce everything, and fix the mind on the Lord".

So, it is very exciting to hear to these eminent persons, these lead-kindly-lights. We are fortunate enough to have many such guiding angels to brighten our paths and direct us in right direction. Needless to say that we commoners may be enthusiastic and are interested to lead a virtuous life and follow an ethically perfect path of actions as administered by all these *jnanis*. But, in reality we are enmeshed and entangled by our own attachments and aversions and many mundane emotional feelings. These feelings overlay and cover the innate Godly and the pious thoughts. They push us into a quagmire of grief and pain due to the feeling of earthly sufferings and gets us into a *moha* or delusion. The following message given by Bhagawaan Sri Krishna in *Aatmasanyama yoga* in Bhagavad Gita is just the absolute truth that one needs to realize:

---

10 *Sri Ramakrishna Paramahamsa* [1836 - 1886]- A great philosopher, a mystic and a yogi; Propagated the message that the ultimate goal of every living soul is God-realization and all faiths are different routes that lead up to a single goal, that is God

उद्धरेदात्मनात्मानं नात्मानमवसादयेत् ।
आत्मैव ह्यात्मनो बन्धुरात्मैव रिपुरात्मनः ॥ ५ ॥

1st sloka - Aatmasanyama yoga

Meaning: Everyone should lift himself by himself. Because, he himself is his friend and he himself may be his enemy also.

बन्धुरात्मात्मनस्तस्य येनात्मैवात्मना जितः ।
अनात्मनस्तु शत्रुत्वे वर्तेतात्मैव शत्रुवत् ॥ ६ ॥

2nd sloka- Aatmasanyama yoga

Meaning: To a person who is in control of his body and sense-organs, feelings and emotions, his own self is a friend, but to a person one who has not conquered himself, his own self acts like an external enemy.

So, what is required here is:

- to make a start in correcting our way of life,
- to muster our inner strength and
- to elevate ourselves to a higher level of understanding,

in order to comprehend / understand our real self and in particular to become aware of the Divine residing within us. Divinity in the form of '*aatma* or *jiva*' resides in every being. *Aatma* is none other than the *amsa* (part) of the Supreme Self and waits to be recognized by us. Whoever is seized of this truth and whoever perceives the same in all beings around is a blessed soul.

With all this turmoil of introspection, one may be often embroiled or confused about the final aspiration in this life. This life even though short and impermanent, has been bestowed on us in precious human form by the benevolent Almighty. Here speaking about myself, I was always tempted to make the following passionate entreaty to *Paramaatma* and my intended appeal to HIM is as follows:

> *O Paramaatma, of janma raahityam I am ignorant,*
> *For this I am eligible or not also, I know not.*
> *Instead, with tears filling my eyes I request thee*
> *to bestow on me a life in human form at least,*
> *I need to spend nine months in darkness though.*

'janma raahityam' in the first line means a state of no further rebirth in this mundane world. At least, I am frank enough to admit in my above appeal that I don't know if I am eligible for this *'janma raahityam'* or not. That is the very reason for my request to *Paramaatma* to bestow on me again a human form, in the next *janma* (next birth) also, so that I can utilize myself to engage in HIS prayers. Even though the request seems to be relevant, one stark truth, we must know. What is it?

Beyond this earthly life and after the final event of leaving this world, there is all stillness or numbness or nothingness - with no knowledge whatsoever of the so-called next destination after that imminent event of death. Then, a thought hovered in my mind: why letting myself bother about what is beyond? I began to feel that it is more prudent and appropriate to prostrate before HIM and make an earnest appeal to HIM to reshape and direct my present life in this birth itself. With this revelation or wise thought, I now wish to make the following entreaty to *Paramaatma*:

> *O Paramaatma, so bless me with YOUR kindness that*
> *I think of YOU only every instant,*
> *I relish in YOUR thoughts only,*
> *I recognize YOU everywhere around,*
> *I perceive YOU in all objects,*
> *I sing in YOUR praise only,*
> *I hear YOU in all sounds with delight and*
> *I care not about the shores beyond this mortal life*

In making my this new and more meaningful appeal to *Paramaatma*, I remind myself and you all with one poem from *Mukundamala stotram* written in Sanskrit by Raja Kulasekhara. Raja Kulasekhara[11] was a saintly king of 9th century and was regarded as one of the Alwars. *Mukundamala* literally means a garland of *slokas* and contains only around forty. Each one of them is a pinnacle or zenith of *bhakti* and also of 'saranagati'. *Saranagati* means a complete surrender to the God Almighty.

Raja Kulasekhara

We find *Mukundamala Stotram* as a unique composition by Raja Kulsekhara. it is unparalleled in any literature for its devotional ecstasy and for the unbounded joy which a devotee derives or develops in expressing his *ananya bhakti* towards the Lord. The particular *sloka* in *Makundamala stotram* which I wish to remind ourselves is:

जिह्वे कीर्तय केशवं मुररिपुं चेतो भज श्रीधरं

पाणिद्वन्द्व समर्चयाच्युत कथाः श्रोत्रद्वय त्वं शृणु ।

कृष्णं लोकय लोचनद्वय हरेर्गच्छांघ्रियुग्मालयं

जिघ्र घ्राण मुकुन्दपाद तुलसीं मूर्धन् नमाधोक्षजम् ॥ १६ ॥

Mukundamala stotram

---

11 Raja Kulsekhara was the earliest king of Chera dynasty in Kerala, India. He was a devotional poet from medieval south India. Kulasekhara was a great devotee of God Vishnu. *Mukundamala stotram*, composed in Sanskrit, is a simple expression of King Kulaśekhara's devotion to Kṛiṣhṇa, the God incarnate in Dwapur yuga.

> **Meaning:** Through this *sloka*, the poet Kulsekhara imploringly reminds himself and earnestly requesting his own *Indriyaas*: i.e., He says: O my Tongue! sing the glories of Bhagawaan Sri Krishna; O my Mind! please remember HIM as the slayer of the *asura* by name Mura and think HIM as the Lord of Shree Lakshmi. O my two Hands! make devout offerings to Him; O my two Ears! please listen to Lord's stories always; O my two Eyes! please behold and see Krishna's Form only; O my two Feet! please go towards Lord's abode – the temple - for worshipping HIM always; my Nose! please smell the *Tulasi* leaf offered at the feet of the Lord; O my Head! please bow in reverence to Lord, the supreme and the divine contemplator.

This earnest entreaty of Raja Kulsekhara is so truthful and mind-searching one that one should have this realization always in one's mind and should cultivate the habit of thinking of *Paramaatma* constantly even while going through her /his actions in this mortal world.

With this meaningful advice coupled with an inner voice, let us also follow what Bhagawaan has said in the following two *slokas* in *Rajavidya Rajaguhya Yoga*. The message in these *slokas* is about great souls who recognize HIM as All Pervading Supreme. It is about these great personalities who worshipped HIM with *ananya bhakti* and always sang in HIS praise.

> महात्मानस्तु मां पार्थ दैवीं प्रकृतिमाश्रिताः ।
>
> भजन्त्यनन्यमनसो ज्ञात्वा भूतादिमव्ययम् ॥ १३ ॥
>
> *Rajavidya Rajaguhya Yoga*
>
> **Meaning:** Great souls of divine nature worship HIM with undisturbed minds. They recognize HIM as the eternal and immortal origin or seed of all beings

सततं कीर्तयन्तो मां यतन्तश्च दृढव्रताः ।
नमस्यन्तश्च मां भक्त्या नित्ययुक्ता उपासते ॥ १४ ॥

Rajavidya Rajaguhya Yoga

Meaning: They worship Him with immense faith and devotion. Bowing down before HIM, they always sing in HIS glory

To be able to sing in praise of *Paramaatma* is a divine quality – a quality that the Divine *Paramaatma* only can bless and bestow on an individual. Singing in *Paramaatma*'s praise and in HIS glory is a pleasure to listen to also. For anyone having a compatible feeling of devotion, it equally infuses in him a Divine feeling of elation and immeasurable pleasure. Then, how much satisfaction, abundant joy and a sense of fulfilment the devout singer himself derives from his singing about the Supreme *Paramaatma*! Singing about *Paramaatma*, the Supreme creator of this world, me, you and all gives immense satisfaction to the devotee. It is the most beautiful way of returning his purest feeling of gratitude to *Paramaatma* in this life itself.

Singing in *Paramaatma*'s praise is itself a meditation on HIM with all fervor and firm conviction. This remarkable capability one gets only with an inherent sublime feeling of *Ananya bhakti*. Can we estimate what *Ananya bhakti* can do? It really gives *ananya* (exclusive) and unbounded or limitless joy to a devotee and mesmerize even *Paramaatma* HIMSELF. The bounty or reward accrued by *Ananya bhakti* is best explained by Adi Sankaracharya in *Sivanadalahari* in one of its *slokas*. *Sivanadalahari* by Adi Sankaracharya is an epitome of prayer or entreaty to *Paramaatma*. It contains hundred *slokas* in Sanskrit and each *sloka* is couched with i.e., imbedded or implied with practical philosophy and wisdom. We find in one of the *slokas*, a remarkable display of pure *bhakti* or devotion and worship by a simple ignorant soul. We cannot but bow down our heads in reverence and admiration to Adi Sankaracharya in enlightening us with such glorious description of a worship that leaves us spell-bound and wonder-struck. That particular *sloka* in *Sivanandalahari* reads as:

Shiva Linga

Adi Sanakarachrya

मार्गा-वर्तित पादुका पशु-पतैर्-अङ्गस्य कूर्चायते
गण्डूशाम्बु-निशेचनं पुर-रिपोर्-दिव्याभिशेकायते
किन्चिद्-भक्शित-मांस-शेश-कबलं नव्योपहारायते
भक्तिः किं न करोति-अहो वन-चरो भक्तावतम्सायते 63

Sivanandalahari

<u>The context in the *sloka*:</u>

Here, the devotee is a hunter in a forest by name, *Kannappa*. He happens to see a '*Shiva Linga*' in the jungle. The form of the *Linga* is symbolic for the formless and omnipresent *Paramaatma*. Being a rustic lad and but having a true concern to worship the Lord, *Kannappa* displays his *bhakti* in the purest form.

Meaning: *Kannappa* cleans the *Linga* with his chappals. He brings mouth-fulls of water from a steam nearby and bathes the *linga*. He then offers the remains of already tasted raw-meat as food to the Lord. Adi Sankaracharya exclaims in the verse: *what-else-display* is the height of devotion!

Through this *sloka*, what Adi Sankaracharya has further conveyed to us is this: For Lord Shiva, *i.e.,* the Lord of all beings, the *Paramaatma*, ordinary *pada rakshas* (chappals) of Kannappa have become the crown. The gargled mouthful of water Kannappa brought, have become the holy water of bath. The left-over pieces of his meat which are already tasted by Kannappa, have become the holy offering to the Lord ! Who is that Lord ?. HE is *Paramaatma*. HE is *Tripurantaka*, the destroyer of three *asuras*. And thus most amazingly, an innocent and ignorant hunter who lives in the forest has become a sovereign devotee, *i.e.,* highest of devotees. What is there in this world that devotion to the Supreme Lord cannot do? This is the inner and the real message conveyed in this magnificent poem by Adi Sankaracharya. It is a superlative and supreme teaching by Adi Sankaracharya on the sublime aspect of *ananya bhakti* and pure devotion!

If we remember, Bhagawaan Sri Krishna in *Rajavidya Rajaguhya yoga* has declared in the following *sloka*:

पत्रं पुष्पं फलं तोयं यो मे भक्त्या प्रयच्छति ।

तदहं भक्त्युपहृतमश्नामि प्रयतात्मनः ॥ २६ ॥

Rajavidya Rajaguhya Yoga

Meaning: *Paramaatma* accepts a leaf, a flower, a fruit or a little water offered with devotion and pure mind

One needs to understand that what is offered is of little importance but how it is offered is far more important, as described by Adi Sankarachrya in the above *sloka* of *Sivanadalahari*. It is *ananya bhakti* and devotion that facilitate a devotee to go near to *Paramaatma* and become dear to HIM.

Friends, we know how *Paramaatma* has been easily mesmerized by singing and writings of many *jnaanis* / devotees in our ancient past and also in our recent past. Meerabai[12], Surdas[13], Bhakta Ramadasu[14] are some of them whose soulful prayers and devotional singing pleased *Paramaatma* so much that HE saved them from their sufferings and provided them HIS shelter and proved what HE has declared in the above *sloka* in *Rajavidya Rajaguhya yoga.*

This book is a tiny attempt to meditate on *Paramaatma* while reminding ourselves of these devout, saintly, righteous and Godly personalities who throughout their lives kept singing in HIS praise and had attained fulfilment. In between my sharing of these thoughts with you all, I tried to supplement the book with some of the songs of these great devotees. In doing so, my intention is to understand and feel how much pleasure, how much rapture, how much ecstasy, how much bliss and contentment they might have got in their lives from their beautiful and melodious musical compositions and singing. It is only, with my interest in speaking about Bhagavad Gita – that too a sort of loud thinking on my part as you can understand – and with an interest in reminding myself with the sublime messages given by Bhagawaan Sri Krishna, that I started this book *"Bhagavad Gita and Ananya Bhakti"* and in the process I happen to share with you the happiness what I got in listening to and closely go through the songs / *bhajans* and poems sung and written in praise of God Almighty by some of the great singers and great personalities.

---

12 Meerabai (1498–1556) was a poet, singer and a devotee of the Lord Krishna. Her songs fully speak of eternal love and peace. Meerabai sung in the glory of her Lord Krishna. She was one of the prominent voices of the Bhakti Movement of her times.

13 Surdas was a 16th-century blind devotional poet and singer, who was known for his works written in praise of Krishna, the supreme lord. He was a devotee of Lord Krishna and he was also a revered poet and singer.

14 *Bhadrachala Ramdasu* [1620-1688] was a saint poet of *Sri Rama* popularly known for his devotional songs written in *Telugu* language and revered for the great *bhakti* content in these songs. He was one of the poet-saints of bhakti movement and a revered composer in the Carnatic music tradition. His compositions are mostly *kirtana* genre.

More than the mere words in these songs and poems, I like you all to grasp their lofty meaning and that innate *bhakti* these personalities had shown in their compositions and singing.

I am sure that readers derive pleasure in reading this book and in reminding themselves with the devotional songs / *bhajans* of the few great devotees whom I could reminisce in this short discussion on Bhagavad Gita and the divine messages given by Bhagawaan Sri Krishna.

If any of the viewpoints penned in this short discourse is incorrect or misinterpreted by me, I apologize for the same and state that it is only due to my ignorance and my limited knowledge on such a sublime subject.

With these words, ends the prelude and thus ends "my humble mind's musings"

Acknowledgements

I humbly acknowledge the benevolent Almighty for the inspiration infused in me throughout the scripting of this volume and write a few words of my devotion towards HIM and HIS GITA.

(Visweswara Rao Gorti)

CHAPTER 1

Bhakti and Worship

Bhagawaan Sri Krishna - Baaro Krishnayya

Before I proceed into the chapter, it is a pleasure to remind ourselves with the devotional song *"Baaro Krishnayya"* written by Kanakadasa[15] (1509-1609), the poet and singer in Kannada language. This particular song is a prayer inviting the Lord Sri Krishna to the devotee's house. The poet is imagining and depicting to us, *i.e.,* showing to us a picture before our eyes, of Lord's coming to the house accompanied by beautiful sounds of HIS ornaments – *"dhimmi dhimmi"* of anklets on HIS feet, the sounds *'kini kini"* of adornments on HIS wrist and accompanied by the melodious voice of HIS flute: The song faithfully replicates / reproduces the deep inner feelings of devotion of Kanakadasa towards *Paramaatma*.

---

15 Kanakadasa was born into a Kannada kuruba family of Baada village, Karnataka, India. He was a philosopher and had written many devotional *kirtanas* / songs in Kannada language. Kanakadasa was a composer of Carnatic music, poet and musician. He was a social reformer also. He is one of the great devotees of Lord Sri Krishna.

ಬಾರೋ ಕೃಷ್ಣಯ್ಯ

ಕೃಷ್ಣಯ್ಯ ಬಾ..ರೋ ಕೃಷ್ಣಯ್ಯ

ನಿನ್ನ ಭಕ್ತರ ಮನೆಗೀ....ಗ ಬಾರಯ್ಯ

ಬಾರೋ ಕೃಷ್ಣಯ್ಯ

ಕೃಷ್ಣಯ್ಯ ಬಾ..ರೋ ಕೃಷ್ಣಯ್ಯ

ಬಾರೋ ನಿನ್ನ ಮುಖ ತೋರೋ

ನಿನ್ನ ಸರಿ ಯಾ..ರೋ ಜಗಧರ

ಶೀಲನೆ.

ಬಾರೋ ಕೃಷ್ಣಯ್ಯ

ನಿನ್ನ ಭಕ್ತರ ಮನೆಗೀ....ಗ ಬಾರಯ್ಯ

ಬಾರೋ ಕೃಷ್ಣಯ್ಯ

ಅಂದುಗೇ ಪಾಡಗವು ಕಾಲಂದುಗೆ

ಕಿರು ಗೆಜ್ಜೆ

ಧಿಮ್ ಧಿಮಿ ಧಿಮಿ ಧಿಮಿ ಧಿಮಿಕೆನುತ

ಪೂಂಗೊಳನೂದುತ ಬಾರಯ್ಯ

ಪೂಂಗೊಳನೂದುತ ಬಾರಯ್ಯ

ಬಾರೋ ಕೃಷ್ಣಯ್ಯ

ನಿನ್ನ ಭಕ್ತರ ಮನೆಗೀ....ಗ ಬಾರಯ್ಯ

ವಾಸ ಉಡುಪಿಲಿ ನೆಲೆಯಾದಿ

ಕೇಶವನೆ

ದಾಸ ನಿನ್ನ ಪದ ದಾಸ

ವಾಸ ಉಡುಪಿಲಿ ನೆಲೆಯಾದಿ

ಕೇಶವನೆ

ದಾಸ ನಿನ್ನ ಪದ ದಾಸ

Kanakadasa

ದಾಸ ನಿನ್ನ ಪದ ದಾಸ ನಿನ್ನ ಪದ ದಾ..ಸ ಬಾರೋ ಕೃಷ್ಣಯ್ಯ ನಿನ್ನ ಭಕ್ತರ ಮನೆಗೀ....ಗ ಬಾರಯ್ಯ ಬಾ..ರೋ ಕೃಷ್ಣಯ್ಯ ಬಾರೋ ನಿನ್ನ ಮುಖ ತೋರೋ ನಿನ್ನ ಸರಿ ಯಾ..ರೋ ಜಗಧರ ಶೀಲನೇ ಬಾ..ರೋ ಕೃಷ್ಣಯ್ಯ ಕೃಷ್ಣಯ್ಯ ಕೃಷ್ಣಯ್ಯ ಬಾ..ರೋ ಕೃಷ್ಣಯ್ಯ	

<u>Thus, the song contains a soulful prayer by Kanakadasa with the following meaning:</u>

O Krishnayya, come to YOUR devotee's house now.

Come, show your face. Who is equal to YOU in this universe?

One who has sandals on his feet and small jingles which are worn on HIS ankles that make the sound *dhimdhimi and dhim dhimmi.*

Come playing YOUR flute to YOUR devotee's house now.

One who has sparkling gold rings and has bangles on his hand that make the sound *kinkini and kini kini.*

Come playing YOUR flute to YOUR devotee's house now.

Oh! Krishnayya, YOU stay in Udupi[16], I am a devotee at YOUR feet, come and protect me.

---

16   Udupi in Karnataka state, India is famous for Sri Krishna temple

Bhakti and Worship

Bhakti may be displayed by *manasaa, vaachaa* and *karmanaa. Manasaa* means by mind, *vaachaa* by words and *karmanaa* by actions. *Bhakti* is a culmination of our expression of devotion to *Paramaatma* by these three modes of *tapas. Tapas* means worship. Bhagawaan Sri Krishna described the worship in the following *slokas* in *Sradhatriya vibhaga yoga*:

देवद्विजगुरुप्राज्ञपूजनं शौचमार्जवम् ।
ब्रह्मचर्यमहिंसा च शारीरं तप उच्यते ॥ १४ ॥

Sradhatriya vibhaga yoga

Meaning: Worshipping the Gods by bodily actions involving physical activity is worship by actions. It also requires purity, straightforwardness and an attitude of *ahimsa, i.e.,* no harm meant to others - on the part of the worshipper

---

अनुद्वेगकरं वाक्यं सत्यं प्रियहितं च यत् ।
स्वाध्यायाभ्यसनं चैव वाङ्मयं तप उच्यते ॥ १५ ॥

Sradhatriya vibhaga yoga

Meaning: Worshipping by words / speech and practice of the study of the Vedas is worship by speech. It also requires the worshipper to be truthful, pleasant and non-offensive to others

---

मनःप्रसादः सौम्यत्वं मौनमात्मविनिग्रहः ।
भावसंशुद्धिरित्येतत्तपो मानसमुच्यते ॥ १६ ॥

Sradhatriya vibhaga yoga

Meaning: Worshipping within the mind with serenity, good heartedness, self-control, purity and silence is worship by mind

---

Understanding these three modes or types of worship is said to be complete if we also grasp the true meaning of what is implied in the above *slokas.* In fact, knowing our limitations and hesitations, Bhagawaan Sri Krishna gave us clarification in this regard. The essence of these worships is contained in the following *sloka* of the same *Sradhatriya vibhaga yoga:*

श्रद्धया परया तप्तं तपस्तत्त्रिविधं नरैः ।
अफलाकाङ्क्षिभिर्युक्तैः सात्त्विकं परिचक्षते ॥ १७ ॥

Sradhatriya vibhaga yoga

Meaning: The threefold worship practiced by steadfast men with utmost faith and with no desire for any reward is called *Saatvic*

Along with this message, we must also remember the caution given by Bhagawaan Sri Krishna in the same *Sradhatriya vibhaga yoga* that many so-called worshippers out of exuberance or excitement may concentrate more on external exhibition of their desire to get recognized by all. These persons are of '*raajasic*' nature. Bhagawaan has also said that those who do worship with haughty nature causing sorrow and discomfort to others and to themselves also are *taamasic* by nature.

So, from this message by Bhagawaan, we need to grasp that in whatever mode one wishes to do worship – by actions or speech or mind - it must be '*saatvic*' that requires the highest level of self-control, faith and serenity. In this much-desired *saatvic* type of *tapas*, *maanasica puja*, *i.e.,* the worship by mind is unique compared to that involving physical activity and speech. The worship by mind may also be regarded as *dhyaana* or meditation.

Adi Sankaracharya amply illustrated the invaluable influence of worship by mind on a devotee in his composition '*Devi Maanasa puja*' written in Sanskrit. In this singular composition, Adi Sankaracharya describes a devotee performing the *Maanasica puja* in his mind imagining the God Almighty in the form of a 'Devi' or Goddess. The devotee obediently and faithfully performs the *sevas* (services) to the Goddess starting from waking her up in the early morning from her sleep. The devotee wakes up the Goddess by singing in her praise and imploring, *i.e.,* pleading HER to cast HER kindliest and benevolent looks and bestow happiness on the whole universe which is waiting on HER. This is best described by Adi Sankaracharya in the first *sloka* of *Devi Maanasa Puja* which reads as:

ఉషసి మాగధమంగలగాయనై:
ర్ఘుటితి జాగృహి జాగృహి జాగృహి
అతికృపార్ధకటాక్షనిటీక్షణై:
జగదిదం జగదంబ సుఖీకురు.. 1..

Devimanasa puja

Adi Sankarachrya

The *maanasica puja* goes forward step by step devotedly and it continues to the next *seva* of offering a golden and jewel-studded throne to the Goddess to get comfortably seated. The whole spectacle of utmost devotion on the part of the devotee in performing the services to the Goddess - one after another performed within his mind - is so enchantingly described by Adi Sankaracharya in *Devi Mansa Puja* that it leaves us enthralled and spellbound. This *saatvic* worship needs a state of vacant mind with all thought process stalled within and it needs the utmost concentration on the part of the devotee converging fully on to the *sevas* being performed by him to *Paramaatma*. This state with a focused and meditative mind, may be described as the one pointed out by *sage* Patanjali[17] in *Samadhi pada* of his *yoga sutra* and the *sutra* is:

---

17 Sage Patajali was a mystic and philosopher in ancient India and an author of several works in Sanskrit. Out of these, the greatest scripture is *Yoga Sutra*, a classical text on *yoga* practice. *yoga sutra* written by the sage in Sanskrit contains four sections or *four padas*. The first section is '*Samadhi pada*'. in which the sage describes the ways to develop concentration, *i.e.,* ways to fix one's mind on *Paramaatma*. *Sutra* means principle or a rule. *Yoga sutra* is a unique composition of sage Patanjali and the *sutras* contained therein are very short and crisp and are also known as aphorisms (dictums).

योगश्चित्तवृत्तिनिरोधः ॥२॥

Yoga sutra

Sage Patanjali

Meaning: The above *sutra* carries the meaning about the necessity for restraining the *Chitta* for concentration, *i.e.* restraining the mind from taking various *Vrittis*. *Vrittis* mean forms and these various forms arise from our thoughts only.

Further comments on Yoga Sutra: Swami Vivekananda[18] in his commentary on Yoga Sutra (Ref: *Patanjali Yoga Sutras by Swami Vivekananda*) very aptly explained about this specific sutra: Suppose that, *Chitta, i.e.,* the mind is a lake and our own true self is at the bottom of the lake. Just as the lake will be clear and the bottom of the lake is visible only when there are no waves, similarly our own true self (lying deep within the *Chitta*) is realized (*i.e.* self-realization will be attained) only when the mind is kept calm and tranquil by 'abhayasa', *i.e.* by practice of concentration and when it is made free from all the '*vrittis*' i.e. thoughts. This is the central meaning contained in the above simple *sutra*.

---

18 *Swami Vivekananda* [1863-1902] – Original name is *Narendranath Datta*; He was the disciple of *Sri* Ramakrishna Paramahams. He addressed the parliament of the World's Religions in Chicago in 1893 and familiarized the western world with *Vedanta* philosophy and *yoga*.

Only a mind of *sankalpa*[19] *rahityam* (*i.e.,* only a mind free of thoughts) is eligible for performing *maanasa puja* and then only, one truly derives the bliss from the worship. Two things stand out here for us to note with utmost attention with regard to *maanasica puja*. One is the aspect of *sankalpa rahityam* and the other is *saguna puja*. As is obvious, *saguna puja* is the worship of the infinite *Paramaatma* in a manifested form.

Sankalpa rahityam

Sankalpa rahityam is attainable by keeping the mind steady in control, *i.e.,* keeping the mind steady by meditation. Towards achieving this, it is needed to keep oneself more calm and strive for self-withdrawal from all the external disturbances while performing worship – *i.e.,* trying to withdraw oneself from all the disturbances and the external attractive or repulsive forces.

For commoners and ordinary mortals like me, lack of control over our thoughts and loss of concentration during our worship are the main obstacles in our path to achieve that blissful state as experienced by a true devotee. Meerabai, Surdas, Annamaya and many devout singers are such worshippers who filled their hearts with that *aatmananda, i.e.,* the eternal bliss during their worship by singing in praise of *Paramaatma*. How much control over their minds and how much dispassionate or detached feeling they must have had towards the external influences / disturbances! With how much endurance and resolution they might have kept their minds away from their sufferings in their lives! It is apt to remember the advice given by Bhagawaan Sri Krishna in the following *sloka* in *Aatmasanyama yoga* about the importance of the much-needed *dhyaana* and practice to attain detachment and to be free from *sankalpaas* (thoughts):

---

19 *Sankalpa* means a thought

असंशयं महाबाहो मनो दुर्निग्रहं चलम् ।
अभ्यासेन तु कौन्तेय वैराग्येण च गृह्यते ॥ ३५ ॥

Aatmasanyama yoga

Meaning: Undoubtedly, the mind is difficult to control and, no doubt, it is restless, but, it can be restrained by practice and by developing a sense of *vairagya*, i.e. detachment.

We also have received a significant message from Bhagawaan Sri Krishna in the same *Aatmasanyama yoga*:

यदा हि नेन्द्रियार्थेषु न कर्मस्वनुषज्जते ।
सर्वसङ्कल्पसन्न्यासी योगारूढस्तदोच्यते ॥ ४ ॥

Aatmasanyama yoga

Meaning: A person is able to control the disturbances caused by the inner thoughts of the mind (*sankalpaa*s) when he is not attached to sense objects and when he is not desirous of results from his actions, *i.e.,* when he becomes a *karma yogi*.

Saguna puja

We are generally given to understand that true Supreme Self, *i.e., Paramaatma* is formless and is '*nirguna*', *i.e.,* HE has no attributes. In this context, the lives of the great *rishis* / sages of ancient past and great philosophers of our times are the direct indicators of the fact that the path to realization of the Infinite Self is arduous - because the aspirant has to practice utmost self-control and he has to renounce the world outwardly and also inwardly. In this regard, the following clarification by Bhagawaan Sri Krishna in *Bhakti yoga* regarding *Saguna puja* or about worshipping *Paramaatma* in a manifested form, *i.e.,* worshipping HIM with a form and attributes is a great revelation.

मय्यावेश्य मनो ये मां नित्ययुक्ता उपासते ।

श्रद्धया परयोपेतास्ते मे युक्ततमा मताः ॥ २ ॥

Bhakti yoga

Meaning: Worship and meditation on a form of an idol or a symbol representing the Infinite Self is a perfect *yoga* when the devotee fixes her / his mind on HIM, worship HIM with all earnestness and Supreme faith.

This message is indeed a great relief to me – a commoner and a mere house-holder. In this context, we also need to remember Bhagawaan's following messages in *Rajavidya Rajaguhya yoga* and *Jnaana vijnaana yoga*.

First if we hear to Bhagawaan's message in Rajavidya Rajaguhya yoga:

ज्ञानयज्ञेन चाप्यन्ये यजन्तो मामुपासते ।

एकत्वेन पृथक्त्वेन बहुधा विश्वतोमुखम् ॥ १५ ॥

Rajavidya Rajaguhya yoga

Meaning: While self-realized *Jnaanis, i.e.,* while *jnaana* yogis worship *Paramaatma* as ONE equal to them and as Formless and Absolute, many others worship HIM in various entities taking HIM to be diverse in the name of manifold divine forms

---

The message in *Jnaana Vijnaana yoga* which is specifically on *nirguna* and *saguna* forms of worship supplements the above message. It also reveals the magnanimity of *Paramaatma* towards HIS devotees who worship HIM by *saguna puja*. This particular *sloka* in *Jnaana Vijnaana yoga* reads as:

यो यो यां यां तनुं भक्तः श्रद्धयार्चितुमिच्छति ।
तस्य तस्याचलां श्रद्धां तामेव विदधाम्यहम् ॥ २१ ॥

Jnaana Vijnaana yoga

Meaning: In whatever form a devotee worships with *sraddha*, *i.e.* faith, *Paramaatma* makes his faith unflinching or unwavering in that form of worship alone.

So it is only the firm conviction and belief with which one meditates on *Paramaatma* – in manifest or unmanifest form - that matters most more than the mode of worship which she / he follows.

Knowing the limitations, imperfections and deficiencies that accompany mere mortals like me, Bhagawaan Sri Krishna is so benevolent. HE is, no doubt, encouraging us to always fix our mind and intellect on HIM while going through our actions, but as a true teacher, HE has also suggested in *Bhakti yoga,* alternative means or different paths of discipline in case of any difficulty to devote fully on HIM. Let us have the fortune of going through this sublime message which is depicted below pictorially.

अथ चित्तं समाधातुं न शक्नोषि मयि स्थिरम् ।
अभ्यासयोगेन ततो मामिच्छाप्तुं धनञ्जय ॥ ९ ॥

Bhakti yoga – 9th sloka

If unable to fix the mind steadily on *Paramaatma*	You do attempt to pray on HIM by yoga of constant practice, for example, by *maanasica puja* on personal God of an individual faith or by practice of meditation. The practice suggested here by Bhagawaan includes practice of pranayama, the practice of constant recitation of *Omkara* or any other Divine name

अभ्यासे ऽप्यसमर्थोऽसि मदर्थमपि कर्माणि भव ।
मत्कर्मपरमो कुर्वन्सिद्धिमवाप्स्यसि ॥ १० ॥

Bhakti yoga– 10th sloka

If unable to seek HIM by above practice	Be intent or concentrate on doing actions for *Paramaatma*'s sake – for example by doing all actions with utmost concentration, reverence and love towards the God Almighty – do all actions whether of charity or service to others in HIS name

> अथैतदप्यशक्तोऽसि कर्तुं मद्योगमाश्रितः ।
> सर्वकर्मफलत्यागं ततः कुरु यतात्मवान् ॥ ११ ॥

Bhakti yoga - 11th sloka

If unable even to follow the above advice

Bhagawaan has suggested in this particular *sloka*: with self-control, do surrender the fruits of all actions – that is, go through any action either stipulated by *Sastraas*, or action connected with an austerity or action connected with a service to others and even a service meant for self to meet one's own bodily needs - do all these actions with a sense of detachment and as a self-less duty - in short - do actions with a feeling of *nishkama karma* - i.e., do actions without expecting anything in return

From the above message, it is for us, mortals to clearly understand that the different means or ways of discipline suggested by *Paramaatma*, are neither inferior nor superior to each other. They merely indicate the ways to attain self-realization or they indicate the ways to attain realization of the true values of this life by different practicants, *i.e.,* different mortals depending on their nature. Also, it is significant to discern or distinguish between these alternative disciplines and in the sequel it is imperative or important to realize Bhagawaan's kindness and consideration towards common mortals like me. Carefully reflecting on Bhagawaan's messages, one may be able to grasp the truth. What is that truth?

Many mortals like me may have no natural or specific love or devotion towards the God Almighty with or without faith on HIS Omnipresence and Omniscience. They may be knowledgeable and may already be aware of the necessity to be virtuous and honest in this short and impermanent life. It is also possible that they know the truth about the right and true purpose in this life, *i.e.,* the truth that we only need to go through all *karmas* (actions) in our lives during our worldly pursuits but we have no right to aspire or desire for the fruits thereof. In fact, this is just the path of discipline based on *nishkaama karma* suggested by Bhagawaan in the last *sloka* (*i.e.,* the 11th *sloka* in *Bhakti yoga* which is rewritten below).

अथैतदप्यशक्तोऽसि कर्तुं मद्योगमाश्रितः ।
सर्वकर्मफलत्यागं ततः कुरु यतात्मवान् ॥ ११ ॥

Bhakti yoga - 11th sloka

We already knew the meaning of this *sloka* earlier – *i.e.,* one must continue to do actions in this life with a feeling of *nishkaama karma, i.e.,* doing actions with no expectation in return. This generous or benevolent message more significantly applies to persons like me who may not entertain any special affinity towards the God Almighty and may not entertain any thoughts about HIM but definitely recognized the precious value of this life in human form. In this context, the *sloka* in *Rajavidya Rajaguhya yoga* is important to remember:

समोऽहं सर्वभूतेषु न मे द्वेष्योऽस्ति न प्रियः ।

ये भजन्ति तु मां भक्त्या मयि ते तेषु चाप्यहम् ॥ २९ ॥

Rajavidya Rajaguhya yoga

Bhagawaan has proclaimed in this *sloka* with the meaning: HE considers all beings same and there is none hateful or dear to HIM. For those who worship HIM with devotion, HE resides in them and they are in HIM.

From this message, we clearly understand that anyone is free to follow his path of discipline based on his nature and create such environment around himself that he possibly discovers the in-dweller, the true self lying within. In any case, for a seeker of truth, besides following any of the above paths of discipline suggested by Bhagawaan, it is wise and prudent to come out of her / his mental shackles or chains and direct herself / himself in developing sincere faith and devotion towards the God Almighty, the creator of this world. This all indicates that one should analyze oneself thoroughly and realize the true-self-within *vis-a-vis* the Supreme Self.

In order to develop devotion towards the Creator of this world and in the process, to appreciate HIS presence in every being / in every object around us, we need to remind ourselves about the significant message received from Bhagawaan Sri Krishna and contained in the following *sloka* of *Kshetra Kshetrajna yoga*:

अविभक्तं च भूतेषु विभक्तमिव च स्थितम् ।
भूतभर्तृ च तज्ज्ञेयं ग्रसिष्णु प्रभविष्णु च ॥ १६ ॥

Kshetra Kshetrajna yoga

Meaning: *Paramaatma* is undivided, yet He exists as if divided among beings – both animate and inanimate; He is Vishnu known as the supporter of beings; He is Siva, the destroyer and HE is Brahma, the creator of all.

As can be inferred from the above *sloka, Paramaatma* is all-pervading and omnipresent. There is no place where HE is not present; Yet, we need to know that HE is *'avyaktam'* meaning unfathomable, incomprehensible and inexplicable. For a devotee, HE is near. HE is far to a non-believer. Here, I recollect a devotional song by Tyagaraja[20] who is fondly known as Tyagayya (1767-1847). He is one of the greatest composers of Carnatic *sangeet* (music) and his songs written in Telugu language are mostly in praise of Sri Rama, the incarnation of the God Almighty in *Treta yuga*. The song speaks well of Tyagayya's unflinching faith and devotion towards *Paramaatma* and it reads as:

---

20 Tyagaraja was born to a Telugu family and he was named Tyagabrahmam / Tyagaraja after Tyagaraja, the presiding deity of the temple at Thiruvarur, the place of his birth. Tyagaraja began his musical training at an early age. Tyagaraja was a saint and composer of Carnatic_music, a form of Indian classical music. He regarded music as a way to experience God's love. His compositions are mainly of a devotional (*bhakti*) or philosophical nature. He composed thousands of devotional *kirtanas* (songs), most of them in praise of Lord Sri Rama. He and his contemporaries Muthuswami Dikshitar and Shyama Shastry are known as the famous Trinity of Carnatic music.

ఎవరని నిర్ణయించిరిరా
నిన్న ఎవరని నిర్ణయించిరిరా
నిన్ం-ఎట్లారాధించిరిరా నర వరుల్
ఎట్లారాధించిరిరా
ఎవరని నిర్ణయించిరిరా
నిన్ం-ఎట్లారాధించిరిరా నర వరుల్
ఎవరని

శివుడనో మాధవుడనో
కమల భవుడనో
పర-బ్రహ్మమనో
ఎవరని నిర్ణయించిరిరా
నిన్ఎవరని నిర్ణయించిరిరా
నిన్ం-ఎట్లారాధించిరిరా నర వరుల్
ఎవరని

శివ మంత్రమునకు మ జీవము
మాధవ మంత్రమునకు రా జీవము
యీ వివరము తెలిసిన ఘనులకు
మొక్కెద వితరణ గుణ త్యాగరాజ
వినుత
నిన్ఎవరని నిర్ణయించిరిరా
నిన్ం-ఎట్లారాధించిరిరా నర వరుల్
ఎవరని

Tyagayya

Meaning: In this specific *Kirtana*, Tyagayya addresses *Paramaatma* and wishes to know:

"Who You are? and the most Eminent people what they decided about YOU?

How these Eminent people imagined YOU to be?

and how did they worship YOU?

– in the form of Lord Siva?

or in the form of *Lord Vishnu*?

or in the form of *Lord Brahma*?

or in the form of *Parabrahma*? i.e., the Supreme Lord of the universe?

The devotee in Tyagayya wishes to know the truth.

He wishes to salute all the great personalities who understood and knew the truth

This above *kirtana* (song) of Tyagayya is an ultimate expression of profound devotion that a person develops towards the Supreme *Paramaatma*. Through the *kirtana*, the intense devotion in Tyagayya conveyed us in a very subtle manner the advice: 'ye ignorant men! perceive *Paramaatma* in every object. Devote on HIM either in *saguna rupa* or *nirguna rupa* – It is nothing but the worship of the Supreme Self and everything converges to HIM".

Ordinary mortals like me leading mundane lives, are often plagued i.e., often troubled by wavering minds and doubts and misgivings: *As a simple house-holder what I can do? Will Paramaatma be satisfied by small prayers of mine?* Many other doubts nag our minds often – as if pricking with a needle. An antidote to all this mental ailment – (Yes.

This is an ailment or sickness. Lack of self-faith is itself an ailment) - is to divert our minds and concentrate on hearing to soulful prayers of these great devotees. Let us remember Sant Tulsidas[21] and hear to what he has said in one of his *dohe*: "

> जे जन रूखे बिषय रस चिकने राम सनेहँ।
> तुलसी ते प्रिय राम को कानन बसहि कि गेहूँ ॥
>
> (*Doha* from Sant Tulsidas Dohavali)

Meaning: Only those who have renounced or forsook or left their attachment to the material gross world of sense objects, *i.e.,* abandoned the desire or longing for the sense objects, and who are instead engrossed or immersed in enjoying the taste of the nectar of love and devotion for Sri Ram, the God incarnate, they are the ones who are the beloved of *Paramaatma* and who are dear to *Paramaatma.*

As we can easily grasp the meaning in the above '*doha*', Sant Tulsidas has cleared the doubt nagging the mind of a commoner like me by a very apt and splendid advice. *He has* said, "For a person with his mind always riveted on *Paramaatma*, it does not matter whether he stays in the forest (as a hermit) or lives as a mere householder".

Tulsidas further said in his *dohe*, "There can be no happiness for a being nor can its mind know any peace even in a dream so long as it does not

---

21   Tulasidas of 15th century was a saint and poet, renowned for his devotion to the deity Rama. He wrote several popular works mostly in Sanskrit and vernacular Awadhi language. He is best known as the author of the *Hanuman Chalisa* and *Ramcharitmanas*. The latter is an excellent reciting in Awadhi language of *Ramayana*. Sant Tulsidas, based on his personal observation of life and the evils afflicting the contemporary society, penned his observations in the form of couplets of two line verses called 'Dohas'. The whole collection is called 'Dohawali' which has around five hundred Dohas that cover a variety of subjects such as *bhakti* i.e., devotion, *Satya* i.e. truth and Dharma, i.e., virtuousness

relinquish desire, which is an abode of sorrow". That is the life of a *nishkama karma yogi* about whom Bhagwaan has advised in the *sloka* of Bhakti yoga (11th *sloka*) which we just remembered about. All these great personalities practiced what they preached to the mankind.

From our side, what is required is to pay heed to the advices given by these *jananis* with full conviction and it is also required to develop self-faith in what we believe and follow.

If we seek for further enlightenment particularly on path of *bhakti* or devotion, we have Narayaneeyam, a remarkable composition by Narayana Bhattari[22] (of 16th century) in Sanskrit. It is considered to be an extraordinary abridgement of Veda Vyasa's Mahabhagavatam. The poet Narayana Bhattatri skillfully encapsulated within only around 1000 *slokas* (in 100 dasakams with approximatey 10 slokas in each) all the essential and central theme contained in Veda Vyasa's magnum opus. Narayaneeyam strengthens and deepens the reader's faith in the basic theme of *bhakti* and its practice in daily life. For instance, it is exhilarating or exciting to hear to some of the *slokas* in Narayaneeyam, particularly those *slokas* describing the mesmerized state of *gopikaas*[23] on hearing to the harmonious flow of musical notes from Krishna's

---

22 Narayana Bhattatri (of 16th century) was born in a Namboothiri family in Kerala, India at a place close to the famous temple at Tirunavayi, on the banks of river Bharatpuzha. He is most famous for his Narayaneeyam, a devotional poem that is still sung at the temple in Guruvayoor where he worked. According to the legend, Narayana's *guru* (teacher) Achyuta Pisharati was struck with paralysis. Unable to see his pain, by yogic strength, Narayana Bhattathri is said to have taken the disease upon himself and relieved his *guru*. Later, he is cured of the disease by the Lord Krishna HIMSELF, after the poet pleased HIM by his *ananya bhakti* through his devotional composition Narayaneeyam.

23 *Gopikaas* are ladies in Gokula village where Krishna grew up and spent HIS youth under the care of HIS foster parents - Nanda and Yashoda. The gopikaas had forsaken everything what they possessed in their lives and adored HIM with all their love. Their love is symbolic of *ananya bhakti.*

flute. The devotion, the *ananya bhakti* and the intense love these *gopikaas* developed towards Krishna have left them in almost a dazed state of not being conscious of their surroundings and their circumstances. Each one of them got swayed away by the magic of the musical waves from the divine flute reaching their ears that compelled them to move towards their beloved Lord posthaste unmindful of in whatever position and wherever they are at that time or whatever family chores they are engaged in.

Tulsidas

The poet Narayana Bhattatri gives a graphic picture of the situation of the *gopikaas* through the following *slokas*:

Om Namo Narayanaya Om Namo Narayanaya

Om Namo Narayanaya

काश्चित्रिजांग परिभूषण मादधाना
वेणुप्रणादमुपकर्ण्य कृतार्धभूषाः ।
त्वामागता ननु तथैव विभूषिताभ्यः
ता एव संरुरुचिरे तव लोचनाय ॥ 65-4

Narayaneeyam

Narayana Bhattatri

Meaning: While some *gopikaas* came to Krishna wearing all their ornaments, some have reached HIM (in a hurry) with incomplete and indecorous or improper fashion. The latter truly delighted Krishna more – obviously! the poet says.

हारं नितम्बभुवि काचन धारयन्ती
काञ्चीश्च कण्ठभुवि देव समागता त्वाम् ।
हारित्वमात्म जघनस्य मुकुन्द तुभ्यं
व्यक्तं बभाष इव मुग्धमुखी विशेषात् ॥   65-5

Narayaneeyam

Meaning: One handsome *gopikaa* came to HIM, wrongly wearing a necklace around her waist instead of decorating her neck with the ornament. It is a magnificent description of her complete engrossment in Krishna's thoughts

The poet Narayana Bhattatri continues to exclaim that those *gopikaas* who could not come to Krishna due to their inability to break away from their family and who instead prayed for HIM in their minds with unflinching faith and adoration and enjoyed the eternal bliss within themselves are indeed the most blessed souls.

When we think of Krishna and gopikaas, it is natural for us to have Gita Govindam of Bhakta Jayadeva[24] coming into our minds. It is one of the famous poems written in Sanskrit by Jayadeva who belonged to second half of 12th century.

Gita Govindam is a *gita* or a song on Govinda that is Sri Krishna. Gita Govindam occupies a unique place as a jewel of philosophical Kirtanas or as a jewel of songs with a strong philosophical tone of superlative splendor and brilliance. The composition is organized into twelve

---

24 Jayadeva is believed to be born in a village called Kindubilva near Puri in Orissa, India. Jayadeva was closely associated with the temple of Jagannatha (temple of Sri Krishna) at Puri, where recitation of his *Gita Govindam* was regularly performed. Songs from the *Gita Govindam* continue to be sung in temples, during festivals. The compositions of Jayadeva profoundly influenced the Indian culture and classical dance forms particularly the Odissi, the traditional classical music of the state Orissa.

chapters. Each chapter is further sub-divided into one or more divisions called *prabandha*s, totaling twenty-four in all.

Jayadeva

The *prabandhas* contain couplets grouped into eights, called *ashtapadis*. *Ashta* means eight. Jayadeva is a great devotee of Sri Krishna and is such a devotee who is the highest among the enlightened *jnaanis* as we can comprehend from his compositions. He has given us and the world a vast panorama of deep and precious philosophical thoughts, through Gita Govinadam. It is replete and filled with all elements of *bhakti rasa* (scented with *sringara bhava – an expression of pure love and longing*). The composition displays exquisite forms of music and dance. Here, we must remember that music and dance are among the different kinds of offerings made to God Almighty in a worship.

Jayadeva through his songs takes us along to a blissful world where *Paramaatma* in the form of Sri Krishna is waiting for his devotee to come to HIM and to get united with HIM – the ultimate goal and aspiration of a devotee.

Here are few lines in one of the most amazing and scintillating *ashtapadi* in Gita Govindam.

Sri Krishna playing flute near Yamuna shore

धीरसमीरे यमुनातीरे वसति वने वनमाली
गोपीपीनपयोधरमर्दनचञ्चलकरयुगशाली ॥ १॥

Gita Govindam

Meaning: In this ashtapadi, Jayadeva is projecting before our eyes an enchanting divine scene: Lord Krishna is waiting in a forest grove on the shore of the Yamuna river with gentle winds blowing around. He waits for his devotee Radha.

Here, Vanamali refers to Lord Krishna. It emphasizes HIS nature affinity through HIS adornment with garlands of forest flowers.

रतिसुखसारे गतमभिसारे मदनमनोहरवेशम् ।
न कुरु नितम्बिनि गमनविलम्बनमनुसर तं हृदयेशम् ॥

Gita Govindam

Meaning: Krishna is decorated with a garland of beautiful flowers. HIS form is scintillating. HE is dressed in the most fascinating attire like the God of sensuality. Radha is asked by her companion to reach the Lord without any delay.

नाम समेतं कृतसंकेतं वादयते मृदुवेणुम् ।
बहु मनुते ननु ते तनुसंगतपवनचलितमपि रेणुम् ॥ २ ॥

Gita Govindam

Meaning: Krishna is softly playing his flute, as if calling HIS devotee by name. The pollen from the flowers has fallen on HIM. HE considers himself greatly fortunate because that pollen must have first touched the body of HIS devotee and come to him by the wind breeze. HE receives them with the utmost honor.

Outwardly, Gita Govindam has a romantic feeling – however, it carries an underlying philosophical connotation or a deep philosophical meaning. It indicates the need for everyone to constantly worship God Almighty and fervently aspire for HIS divine grace with full zeal. The romantic tone of the poem is contained in the description of the eternal love between Lord Krishna and his devotee Radha. The underlying philosophical tone - one can interpret like this: - The *jiva* in a soul when separated from *Paramaatma*, the Supreme Self, suffers from the highest pangs or pains of separation. By the grace of the Lord, the *jiva* when finally finds union with the Lord, will derive unbounded joy and happiness. Here in the song, Krishna is *Paramaatma*, Radha is the *Jivaatma* who longs, *i.e.,* who fervently desires for reunion with her Lord. Thus, Gita Govindam is all about the sacred relationship between a *jiva* and *Paramaatma* and it is about the devotional experience enjoyed by the *jiva* and its blissful union with *Paramaatma.*

We need to understand that these great personalities Jayadeva, Annamaya, Tyagayya are all God's creation of extraordinary geniuses. This aspect reminds us of the message given by Bhagwaan Sri Krishna in the *sloka* of Vibhuti Yoga:

> यद्यद्विभूतिमत्सत्त्वं श्रीमदूर्जितमेव वा।
>
> तत्तदेवावगच्छ त्वं मम तेजों ऽशसम्भवम् ॥ ४१ ॥
>
> *Vibhuti yoga*
>
> **Meaning:** Whatever that is glorious, prosperous or powerful in a being, it is a manifestation of a part of HIS splendor.

So, what is most revealing from this message by Bhagawaan is that while all beings – animate or inanimate - are supported by *Paramaatma* equally, the things of beauty, splendor or extraordinary skill stand for HIS amazing creation and a part of HIS grandeur.

Referring back to Narayaneeyam, we find that the poet Narayana Bhattri assiduously or persistently proclaimed the truth that – *ananya bhakti* and intense love for *Paramaatma* lead a person to divinity. He stressed that in the quest for salvation, the path of devotion is recommended by great sages of our past to be far more superior to *karma yoga* (path of action) and *jnaana yoga* (path of spiritual knowledge). *Karma Yoga* yields results in the distant future and *Jnaana Yoga* is beyond the comprehension of ordinary mortals like me and therefore, it is more prudent to adopt the path of *bhakthi*, the poet Narayana Bhattri says. Entertaining *ananya bhakti* and devotion towards HIM is far more satisfying and soothing to a devotee. The following *sloka* reveals the poet Narayana Bhattri's conviction in this regard.

त्वद्भक्तिस्तु कथारसामृतझरीनिर्मज्जनेन स्वयं
सिद्ध्यन्ती विमलप्रबोधपदवीमक्लेशतस्तन्वती ।
सद्यस्सिद्धिकरी जयत्ययि विभो सैवास्तु मे त्वत्पद-
प्रेमप्रौढिरसार्द्रता द्रुततरं वातालयाधीश्वर ॥   2-10

Narayaneeyam

Meaning: O! Lord Krishna ! *Bhakthi* is the most superior path to merge with YOU and leads us to the state of pure divinity without delay. I pray YOU to grant me the ability to be steeped in devotion to YOUR lotus feet

पठन्तो नामानि प्रमदभरसिन्धौ निपतिताः
स्मरन्तो रूपं ते वरद कथयन्तो गुणकथाः ।
चरन्तो ये भवतास्त्वयि खलु रमन्ते परममू-
नहं धन्यान् मन्ये समधिगतसर्वाभिलषितान् ॥   3-1

Narayaneeyam

Meaning: O! Bestower of boons! Those devotees who constantly sing in YOUR praise, and in YOUR names and who worship YOUR divine form have all their righteous wishes fulfilled by YOU and they are indeed the most blessed souls.

Here, we need to remember the message given by Bhagawaan Sri Krishna in the two *slokas* of *Bhakti yoga*:

ये तु सर्वाणि कर्माणि मयि सन्त्यस्य मत्पराः ।
अनन्येनैव योगेन मां ध्यायन्त उपासते ॥ ६ ॥
तेषामहं समुद्धर्ता मृत्युसंसारसागरात् ।
भवामि नचिरात्पार्थ मय्यावेशितचेतसाम् ॥ ७ ॥

Bhakti yoga – slokas 6 and 7

> **Meaning:** A devotee who renounces all actions in HIM, regards HIM as the Supreme goal and thus who meditates and worships HIM with *ananya bhakti* will be saved by *Paramaatma* HIMSELF from their mortal limitations

If we recollect, Bhagawaan Sri Krishna has said in the following *sloka in Jnaana Vijnaana yoga:*

चतुर्विधा भजन्ते मां जनाः सुकृतिनोऽर्जुन ।
आर्ती जिज्ञासुरर्थार्थी ज्ञानी च भरतर्षभ ॥ १६ ॥

Jnaana Vijnaana yoga

– about which we already reminded ourselves earlier in the prelude. In this *sloka*, Bhagawaan indeed gave specific clarification about four types of *bhaktaas* (worshippers). HE has said that all of them are noble and upright. By this message, what we need to understand is that those worshippers seeking wealth or those seeking relief from distress or those going in pursuit of knowledge are on the right path, *i.e.,* on the path to reach the final desired higher state of a *Jnani,* the fourth type of worshippers. Thus, the former three types of worshippers are elevating themselves step by step from *sakama bhaktaas* (worshippers with desires) to *nishkaama bhaktaas* (worshippers with no desires). Here we are also required to remind ourselves of the advice given by Sri Ramakrishna Paramahamsa to achieve the transformation from *sakaama bhaktaa to nishkaama bhaktaa.* He has advised us: i) to keep engaged in chanting *Paramaatma*'s name and singing in HIS praise, ii) to get always engaged in holy company of righteous persons, iii) to keep aloof whenever possible and think of *Paramaatma* only iv) to develop strong conviction that *Paramaatma* is 'sat', *i.e.,* real and all else 'asat', *i.e.,* unreal and v) to perform the worldly actions in the name of *Paramaatma.*

With this inspirational advice in mind, we go into the next chapter – *Worship and Saranagati*. In our context, *Saranagati* means 'making an intense plea / intense request to *Paramaatma* to grant us HIS shelter'.

CHAPTER 2

Bhakti and *Saranagati*

Sri Krishna - భజరే గోపాలం, మానస భజరే గోపాలమ్

Before I proceed into the chapter, let me remind us all about the devotional song "భజరే గోపాలం, మానస భజరే గోపాలమ్" written by Sadasiva Brahmendra[25], the poet-singer in Telugu language. Sadasiva Brahmendra is a saintly poet (15-16th century), became a worshipper of *Paramaatma* and a saint at very early age. In addition to being an Advaita* philosopher, he was also great composer of Carnatic music and he was indeed a poet composer. Few of his compositions which are available are recognized as the greatest compositions of Carnatic music.

* Advaita philosophy, which towers over all other systems of philosophy, was built by Adi Shankaracharya in the eighth century and it is about the non-dual nature of Brahman as the ultimate Reality.

---

25 Sadasiva was born in a Telugu family in Andhra Pradesh, India. His initial name was Sivaramakrishna. He left his home in search of Truth at a young age and took *Sanyasa* (renunciation). He became the disciple of Sri Paramasivendra Saraswati (57th Shankaracharya of Shri KanchiKamakotiPeetham). After leaving his teacher, he left the formalities of the material life and started moving around stark naked and became reclusive. He reached a state of enjoying the bliss of *Aatma Jnana* (self-realization).

భజరే గోపాలం, మానస భజరే గోపాలమ్ ॥

భజ గోపాలం భజితకుచేలం

జగన్మూలం దితిసుత కాలమ్ ॥

ఆగమసారం యోగవిచారం

భోగశరీరం భువనాధారమ్ ॥

నతమందారం నందకిశోరం

హతచాణూరం హంసవిహారమ్ ॥

Sadasiva Brahmendra

<u>This beautiful song carries the following Meaning:</u>

O Mind!– Worship Gopala (Krishna the cowherd, the protector of cows).

Worship Gopala,– who is the one worshipped by Kuchela, who is the root cause of the three worlds and the annihilator, i.e., destroyer of the *Asuras*, the sons of Diti.

— Worship HIM, who is the child of Nandagopa, who killed the wrestler Chanuraa (in the court of the wicked king Kamsa) and who is the one sporting in the company of *Paramahamsas* or *rishis* or sages, the supreme saintly personalities

<u>Further comments:</u>

As we can understand and relish, Sadasiva Brhamendra's *Kirtanas* or songs are sweetly lyrical. These *Kirtanas* remained as indicative of the heavenly fragrance of the highest Sublime Self. It is the shortness of his *Kirtanas,* their naturalness and their genuine lyrical feeling that touches the inner depths of a soul who is able to vibrate with the same emotion as the poet.

Bhakti and Saranagati

With this fragrance of the above song lingering in our minds, let us go into the chapter.

Ananaya bhakti and *saranagati* are inseparable, as we can easily comprehend. Here, *Saranagati* means a state of mind where one thinks of fully surrendering to *Paramaatma* and desperately seeking for HIS grace. Complete faith on *Paramaatma* is possible only when one devotes on HIM with no attachments and when the mind is fully pervaded by HIM. This in turn leads the devotee to totally surrender herself / himself to *Paramaatma* in both mind and spirit. This is what has been projected before us by Veda Vyasa and Pothana via the episode of *Gajendra moksham* in Mahabhagavatam. In this context, it is very reassuring to have the following message from Bhagawaan Sri Krishna in *Vibhuti yoga* about the devotees who surrender their lives to HIM with their minds always fixed on HIM.

> मच्चित्ता मद्गतप्राणा बोधयन्तः परस्परम् ।
> कथयन्तश्च मां नित्यं तुष्यन्ति च रमन्ति च ॥ ९ ॥
>
> *Vibhuti yoga*

Meaning: Devotees derive immense satisfaction in surrendering to *Paramaatma*. With their thoughts fixed in HIM, they always think of HIM, speak of HIM and enlighten others also about HIM

Surrendering to *Paramaatma* further enlightens the devotee with the revelation that everything belongs to HIM and she / he needs to perform actions for the sake of HIM only, with utmost faith and reverence. The assurance given by Bhagawaan Si Krishna in the following *sloka* in *Rajavidya Rajaguhya yoga* is also significant:

अपि चेत्सुदुराचारो भजते मामनन्यभाक् ।
साधुरेव स मन्तव्यः सम्यग्व्यवसितो हि सः ॥ ३० ॥

Rajavidya Rajaguhya yoga

Meaning: Bhagawaan assures in this *sloka* that even though a person is most sinful but if she / he worships HIM with unflinching or unswerving devotion, she / he must be regarded as righteous and is on the right path to self-realization

Thus, we had clarification from Bhagawaan that the reformed sinner surely becomes virtuous, attains unshakable peace and will never perish. The significance of the above *sloka* is apparent. The effect of single-minded devotion to *Paramaatma* is reiterated. Further, when one recognizes her / his folly while leading this mortal life, corrects herself / himself and devotes unwaveringly on *Paramaatma*, that human personality comes under the protection of the Supreme Divine and gets steered away from the destructive nature of the adverse inclinations. If we hear to the prayers of many devotees, we invariably find their earnest requests to *Paramaatma* for forgiveness and mercy and seeking for HIS protection.

Dhurjati[26], a saintly poet of 16th Century in one of his poems in *Sri Kalahastiswara satakam* written in Telugu language has expressed his remorse for his past actions. In a very poignant and soul-touching manner he prays for HIS pardon. The poem reads as:

26　Dhurjati was born in Srikalahasti, Andhra Pradesh, India. He was a Telugu poet and known as one of 'Ashtadiggajas' (one of eight eminent poets) in the royal court of the great Emperor Krishnadevaraya of Vijayanagara empire in South India. The poet's famous works include the *Sri Kalahasteeshwara Mahatyam* (meaning -The glory of the Lord of Srikalahasti'). In the words of the King Sri Krishnadevaraya, a great poet by himself – "the sweetness of the words of Dhurjati create a melody miracle!"

మ|| వెనుకం జేసిన ఘోరదుర్దశల
భావింపంగ
రోతయ్యెడున్
వెనుక నుందట వచ్చు దుర్మరణముల్
వీక్షింప
భీతయ్యెడున్
నను నే జూచియు నా విధుల్
దలచియున్ నాకే
భయంబయ్యెడున్
జెనకు జీకటి మాయె గాలమునకున్
శ్రీకాళహస్తీశ్వరా!   76

Dhurjati

Poem from Kalahastiswara satakam

Meaning: The poet very sorrowfully says: If I remember my previous vicious and evil deeds, I despise, *i.e.,* hate myself. When I see people dying some on yesterdays and some before, I am getting afraid. When I introspect myself and when I think of my actions, I feel more panicky. I am at a loss to know the way to get rid of this fear. In these final days of my life, I am surrounded by dark clouds of my ignorance. O my Lord, kindly save me.

This is an entreaty from the poet Dhurjati, completely surrendering himself to God Almighty and it is a fervent appeal to save him from his fears about this mortal life.

Surdas who also belongs to 16th Century and who was a revered poet and singer was blind by birth and begged for his alms from door-to-door on the banks of Yamuna river while mesmerizing the people around in his times, with his heart-melting *bhajans* on Sri Krishna. How much fortunate those people must be to have Surdas in their midst and hear to his soulful *bhajans* of intense love towards *Paramaatma*!. In the following *bhajan* / song of Surdas, we will be overwhelmed by the tone of surrender and his sincere request for absolution or forgiveness.

प्रभु मोरे अवगुण चित ना धरो,
समदर्शी है नाम तिहारो,
चाहो तो पार करो,
प्रभु मोरे अवगुण चित ना धरो

इक लोहा पूजा में राखत,
इक घर बधिक परौ।
सो दुबिधा पारस नहिं जानत,
कंचन करत खरौ ॥
प्रभु मोरे अवगुण चित ना धरो

इक नदिया इक नार कहावत,
मैलौ नीर भरी।
जब मिलि गए तब एक-वरन है,
सुरसरि नाम परौ ॥
प्रभु मोरे अवगुण चित ना धरो

तन माया जो ब्रह्म कहावत,
सूरसू मिल बिधारो,
के इनको नीरधार कीजिये,
कई पण जात तारो,
प्रभु मोरे अवगुण चित ना

Surdas

Meaning: O Lord! please ignore my misdoings / faults. You are known as impartial and known to love everyone equally, If you wish then, kindly bestow YOUR grace upon me.

There is a pious iron that is used in the holy worships while there is another that lies with a brutal butcher. O Lord! YOU are like that magical "Paras" stone that is characterized by its holy quality of turning all ferrous objects without differentiating, to pure gold simply by a touch.

On one side there is a river and on another there is a gutter filled with dirty water. When both of them meet together with Ganga, they both are known as Ganga, the holy river. Ganga *Mata* doesn't differentiate between the two.

There is one entity known as *maya* (delusion), and another entity known as 'Brahma' (*i.e, aatma* within a being or the soul-within which is pure). *Aatma* under the impact of *maya* it cannot reach God by itself,. There is so much difference of opinion, O Lord, I am confused and I am dependent on YOU for YOUR mercy. This time, don't delay it! I can't cross this ocean of this material world by myself without YOUR grace.

When a sincere devotee like Surdas compares himself with a valueless iron knife of a butcher and feels that he is unholy as water in a gutter, the simple mortals ignorant like me, what they need to feel of themselves! Surdas even stressed in the song about the wily or devious impact of *moha* or *maya* or *delusion* on a human being. About this vital aspect of *moha*, we have already been made aware of by Bhagawaan Sri Krishna from HIS message in *jnaana vijnaana yoga*:

इच्छाद्वेषसमुत्थेन द्वन्द्वमोहेन भारत।
सर्वभूतानि सम्मोहं सर्गे यान्ति परन्तप ॥ २७ ॥

Jnaana Vijnaana yoga

Meaning: Due to the qualities of desire and anger inherent in mortals, they fall prey to the twin effects of sorrow and happiness leading to *moha* or delusion.

In the same *Jnaana Vijnaana yoga*, Bhagawaan has further said that virtuous persons who are freed from their sins, win over *moha* and they worship and pray for HIM with all steadfastness and faith. The specific *sloka* reads as:

येषां त्वन्तगतं पापं जनानां पुण्यकर्मणाम् ।
ते द्वन्द्वमोहनिर्मुक्ता भजन्ते मां दृढव्रताः ॥ २८ ॥

Jnaana Vijnaana yoga

Meaning: Those persons who follow path of virtuous deeds with *ananya bhakti* get freed from sins and also they are freed from *moha* (delusion) of the pairs of opposites – like happiness and sorrow - born out of desire and anger. They always worship HIM with a firm resolve.

For commoners like us, the beautiful and scintillating *bhajans / kirthanas* of these devotees – whether of joyous or grievous tone - are the source of inspiration and also they are the motivating force for us to develop faith and love towards *Paramaatma*, the *Parama Purusha* and the Supreme Self. We will be overwhelmed to imagine how much unflinching faith and undaunted devotion they must have had towards *Paramaatma* and how much happiness and joy they might have derived in their singing in HIS praise. If we are able to resonate along with them, hearing to their songs will certainly generate - if not to same level

– similar joy or elation in us. It is also gratifying and heartwarming to find these devotees trying all throughout their lives to reform and refine others through their compositions to develop love and affection towards *Paramaatma*, the Creator of this universe.

The following song by Annamaya is an earnest prayer to *Paramaatma* requesting for HIS shelter and protection. It is one of Annamaya's extraordinary compositions and it amply speaks of the poet's divine vision. It makes a great imprint in our minds to realize the truth that *Paramaatma* is the very embodiment of supreme bliss and it is realized only by constant and unfaltering devotion.

నీకే శరణు నీవు నన్నుఁ గరుణించు

యీకడ నాకడ దిక్కు యొవ్వరున్నా
రిఁకను

కన్నులఁ జంద్రసూర్యులుగల వెలుపవు
నీవు

పన్ని నలక్ష్మిభూమిపతివి నీవు

అన్నిఁటా బ్రహ్మకుఁ దండ్రియైన
యాదివెలుపవు

యొన్నఁగ నీకంటే మన మెవ్వరున్నా
రిఁకను

నీకే శరణు

Annamaya

దేవతలందరు నీ తిరుమేనైనమూర్తి
ఆవలఁ బాదాన లోక మణచితివి
నీవొక్కఁడవే నిలిచిన దేవుఁడవు
యెవేళ నీకంటె నెక్కుడెవ్వరున్నా
రిఁకను

నీకే శరణు
అరసి జీవులకెల్ల నంతరాత్మవైన హరి
సిరుల వరములిచ్చె శ్రీవేంకటేశ
పురుషోత్తముఁడవు భువనరక్షకుఁడవు
యిరవైన నీవే కాక యెవ్వరున్నారిఁకను
నీకే శరణు

Meaning: Annamaya says in this *kirtana*: I submit myself to you seeking your shelter and compassion. YOU are the saviour to me and there is nobody else to protect me.

YOU are the Supreme god with the sun and moon deities within YOUR eyes. YOU are the *adi purusha, i.e,* YOU are the beginning and father of Brahma. There is nobody else to protect me.

I submit myself to you seeking your shelter and compassion.

All deities reside in YOURSELF. YOU only are the shield for all. There is nobody else to protect me.

I submit myself to you seeking your shelter and compassion.

YOU are the in-dweller of all beings. YOU are Sri Venkatesa and the bestower of boons. YOU are *Purushottama* and the protector of all. There is nobody else to protect me.

I submit myself to you seeking your shelter and compassion.

As we can comprehend from this song, Annamaya displayed so uniquely his unfailing and abiding faith in Lord Venkateswara, the God incarnate.

Same tone of unbounded reverence and *ananya bhakti* we find in Bhakta Ramadasu who belongs to 17th century and who has shown his irrefutable / undisputable faith through his poems, on Sri Rama, the *Paramaatma's* incarnation in *Treta yuga,*. In one poem in *Dasarathi satakam* written by Ramadasu in Telugu language, he laments that *Paramaatma* only can save him from his sins and give him shelter.

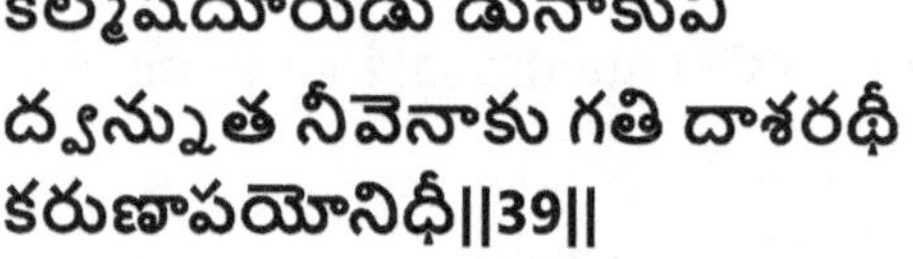

Bhakta Ramadasu

Meaning: Oh! Lord! Sri Rama! Kindly listen to my appeal. There is nobody more wicked than myself in this world. And also there is nobody among the celestials more powerful than YOURSELF and there is nobody more steadfast in driving away the sins of the distressed. Therefore YOU only are my saviour and I take refuge in YOU only and in nobody else.

The word *Dasaradhi* stands for Sri Rama who incarnated in *Treta yuga* taking the form as son of Dasaradha, the king of Ayodhya. The poet in every poem of *Dasarathi satakam* hails Sri Rama as '*karunapayonidhi*' which means 'ocean of compassion'. In another soul-touching poem, the poet Ramadasu brings out his inner thoughts about the final event of death and his sincere and sorrowful wish about the need to pray and surrender to *Paramaatma* that instant itself.

ముప్పైన గాలకింకరులు ముంగిటవచ్చిన వేళ, రోగముల్
గొప్పెరమైనచో గళము కుత్తుక నిండినవేళ, బాంధవుల్
గప్పినవేళ, మీస్మరణ గల్గునొ గల్గదో నాటి కిప్పుడే
తప్పకచేతు మీభజన దాశరథీ కరుణాపయోనిధీ||16||

Dasarathi satakam by Bhakta Ramadasu

<u>Bhakta Ramadasu with so much sorrow and sadness says:</u> In my old age when the messengers of God of death are waiting outside and when the diseases afflicting me aggravate and cause *kapham* (phlegm) to choke my voice and when I am surrounded by relatives, I don't know if I will be in a position to pray. Therefore, O! Lord! I pray now itself.

Referring to all ignorant householders like me, Sri Ramakrishna Paramahamsa says (Sri Sri Ramakrishna Kathamrita-I) that one should hold with one hand the lotus feet of God in surrender and with the other hand has to perform his worldly duties. He further proclaims that when all the responsibilities are fulfilled and when the stage of retirement comes, the householder should hold with both hands the feet of the Lord for HIS supreme shelter. How much true it is! In fact, Sri Ramakrishna Paramahamsa just echoed what Bhagawaan Sri Krishna has said in the following *sloka* in *Mokshasanyasa yoga*:

चेतसा सर्वकर्माणि मयि सन्न्यस्य मत्परः ।
बुद्धियोगमुपाश्रित्य मच्चित्तः सततं भव ॥ ५७ ॥

Mokshasanyasa yoga

Meaning: Bhagawaan urges us to mentally dedicate all our actions to HIM and follow *karma yoga* maintaining even-mindedness, getting solely dedicated to HIM and fixing the mind constantly on HIM

Having the purport of the above divine advice carefully stored in our minds, we proceed to the next chapter *"Bhakti and Agony"*.

CHAPTER 3

Bhakti and Agony

Sri Krishna and gopikaas - నీ దయ రాదా

Before I proceed into the chapter, I wish to recollect and bring to your attention the most heart-rending devotional *kirtana* (song) - నీ దయ రాదా - by Tyagayya written in Telugu language. While yearning for Sri Rama's grace, Tyagayya laments and expresses his unbearable agony through the *kirtana*, "I fully realized that none except you can save me from my sorrow. My mind is going through ceaseless struggle silently. Why, Rama, YOU are delaying to respond to my prayers?"

నీ దయ రాదా,
రామ రామ రామ నీ దయ రాదా
కాదనే వారెవరు కల్యాణ రామ
నీ దయ రాదా
నన్ను బోచువారిలను నాడే తెలియ
ఇన వంశ తిలక నీకింత తామసమా
నీ దయ రాదా
అన్నిటికినధికారుడని నే పొగడితే
మన్నించితే నీదు మహిమకు తక్కువా
నీ దయ రాదా
రామ రామ రామ త్యాగరాజ హృత్-
సదన
నా మది తల్లడిల్లె న్యాయమా వేగమే
నీ దయ రాదా

Tyagayya

<u>Meaning:</u>

Do I not have YOUR benevolence? Oh Sri Rama!

Who obstructs YOU ? Do I not have YOUR benevolence?

I need YOUR protection. Jewel of *Raghu Vamsa*! Why YOU delay in coming to my rescue?

Do I not have YOUR benevolence?

When I adore YOU as the supreme being, why do YOU think it is beneath YOUR dignity to extend YOUR grace to me?

Do I not have YOUR benevolence?

Is it fair of YOU to watch the ceaseless struggle going on in my mind silently?

Oh! Merciful Lord Sri Rama!

Do I not have YOUR benevolence?

It is a melodious song with such a strong sorrowful tone that it fills our minds, as if we also along with Tyagayya are appealing to Paramaatma for HIS grace and kindness. If we now proceed into the chapter:

Bhakti and Agony

Ananya bhakti more often leads to moments of sorrow and unbearable pain or agony to a devotee. The most enchanting episode in *Mahabhagavatam* of Veda Vyasa (Chapter 30, Canto10) concerning g*opikaas* and their devotion towards Krishna amply illustrates how *ananya bhakti* in a devotee leads to deep aspiration for union with *Paramaatma* always. Besides, it also reveals how *ananya bhakti* inflicts or causes agonizing pain and sorrow due to a separation from HIM. We find Veda Vyasa picturesquely describing the event when the *gopikaas* are caught in a state of utter gloom due to their separation from their beloved Krishna. They totally surrender themselves to the Lord in the end. In fact, Krishna, perceiving the *gopikaas*' pride and a feeling of impudence / insolence in them about having HIM in their possession, played the divine act of disappearing from their presence in order to chasten them of their ego and make them realize the truth. Pure devotion and total surrender only tie *Paramaatma* to a worshipper. Later, the *gopikaas*, having been mellowed down by their remorse and having been cleansed of their proud attitude, they began pouring out their prayers in right earnest with a request for a union with their Lord. To our immense fortune, the following few *slokas* in *Mahabhagavatam* abundantly illuminate us about how *ananya bhakti* propel pure devotees to open their hearts out and pour out their innate zeal for a reunion with the Supreme Self.

दृष्टो वः कच्चिदश्वत्थ

प्लक्ष न्यग्रोध नो मनः

नन्दसूनुर्गतो हत्वा

प्रेमहासावलोकनैः

MahaBhagavatam

Meaning: The *gopikas* are asking *asvattha* (fig) and *nyagrodha* (banyan) trees if they have seen Krishna who is the son of Nanda *maharaj* and who has gone away after stealing their minds with HIS loving smiles and glances.

Veda Vyasa

मालत्यदर्शि वः कच्चिन्

मल्लिके जातियूथिके

प्रीतिं वो जनयन् यातः

करस्पर्शन माधवः

MahaBhagavatam

Meaning: When they had no reply from the trees, the *gopikas* question the different jasmine flowers whether Divine Krishna has gone by their side. Because, they thought that HE definitely might have given immense pleasure to them with the touch of HIS hand.

<table>
<tr><td>

किं ते कृतं क्षिति तपो बत केशवाङ्घ्रि-
स्पर्शोत्सवोत्पुलकिताङ्गन हैर्विभाप्ति
अप्यङ्घ्रिसम्भव उरुक्रमविक्रमाद्वा
आहो वराहवपुषः परिरम्भणेन

MahaBhagavatam

</td><td></td></tr>
<tr><td>

Meaning: The *gopikas* even asked the mother earth if she had_seen Lord Krishna passing by her side. They observed that the mother earth appeared beautiful and it must be because of the touch of the beautiful feet of Lord Krishna. They also exclaimed whether that grandeur was of earlier touch by the Lord during HIS incarnations as Vamana or Varaha.

</td><td></td></tr>
</table>

Veda Vyasa in describing the profound sorrow of *gopikass* has expressed in a subtle way, *Paramaatma*'s integral divinity and HIS omnipresence through the above *slokas* - it is indeed the purport contained in each and every *sloka* of Maha Bhagavatam.

Veda Vyasa gave a similar description in Maha Bhagavatam (Chapter 30, Canto10) of the profound sorrow of the *gopikas* at the time when Krishna leaves Brindavan and departs to Madhura. They became very sad and they expressed their sorrow. Their eyes were thirsty for a glance of the Lord. They liked to see Lord's lotus eyes always. They wished to have Krishna who has a mark of saffron on forehead and wears the necklace of pearls, for themselves and got frightened at the prospects of even the briefest separation from their beloved Krishna. The following slokas speak out the gopikaas' agony arising out of their ananya bhakti:

गतिं सुललितां चेष्टां

स्निग्धहासावलोकनम्

शोकापहानि नर्माणि

प्रोद्दामचरितानि च

MahaBhagavatam

Meaning: The *gopikaas* were frightened at the prospect of even the briefest separation from Lord Mukunda (Krishna). So, they began to remember HIS graceful gait, HIS pastimes, HIS affectionate, smiling glances, HIS heroic deeds and HIS playful words, which would relieve their distress

चिन्तयन्त्यो मुकुन्दस्य

भीता विरहकातराः

समेताः सङ्घ‍शः प्रोचुर

अश्रुमुख्योऽच्युताशयाः

MahaBhagavatam

Meaning: The *gopikaas* were beside themselves with anxiety at the thought of the great separation about to come. They gathered in groups and spoke to one another, their faces covered with tears and their minds fully absorbed in *Acyuta* (Krishna).

एवं ब्रुवाणा विरहातुरा भृशं

व्रजस्त्रियः कृष्णविषक्तमानसाः

विसृज्य लज्जां रुरुदुः स्म सुस्वरं

गोविन्द दामोदर माधवेति

MahaBhagavatam

> **Meaning**: The ladies, who were so attached to Krishna, felt extremely agitated by their imminent separation from Him. They forgot all shame and loudly cried out, "O Govinda! O Damodara! O Madhava!"

It is surprising to reminisce or remember that all great devotees like Surdas, Meerabai and many others whose lives we know about, have developed and exhibited same devotion towards Krishna as *gopikaas* in Brindavan, even amidst physical sufferings and utmost personal sorrow. It is equally surprising to know that they in fact derived immense happiness and satisfaction from their singing and compositions, with least regard to their personal predicaments or worries. How much mental strength and how much faith they might have developed towards *Paramaatma* and how much endurance they might have had and with how much sagacity or wisdom they maintained their balance of mind in producing such melodious and blissful compositions in praise of the beloved God. One may invariably find in most of their songs tinges of sorrowful tone indicating their innermost feelings of craving or desire to get near to HIM and get united with HIM. Let us hear to one of the scintillating songs of Surdas on Lord Sri Krishna.

हरी दर्शन की प्यासी,
अखियाँ हरी दर्शन की प्यासी,
देखयो चाहत कमाल नयन को,
निसदीन रहेत उदासी
अखियाँ हरी दर्शन की प्यासी
केसर तिलक मोतिन की माला,
वृंदावन के वासी,
नेह लगाए त्याग गये त्रिन्सम,
डाल गये गाल फाँसी
अखियाँ हरी दर्शन की प्यासी

Surdas

<table>
<tr><td>

काहु के मान की को जानत,

लोगन के मन हासी,

सूरदास प्रभु तुम्हरे दरस बिन,

लेहो करवट काशी

अखियाँ हरी दर्शन की प्यासी

</td><td></td></tr>
</table>

Meaning: Surdas says in this song: For a glimpse of Krishna, my eyes are thirsty (my eyes are craving for). I wish to see the lotus-eyed Krishna. Not seeing HIM makes me restless everyday.

My eyes are thirsty for HIM who wears a saffron *tilak*, and a string of pearls and who lives in *Brindavan*, After stealing my heart, HE forsook me or left me like a worthless blade of grass.

My pain from separation from Krishna, nobody can understand and all making fun of me. O! Krishna ! without seeing you, I cannot rest. My eyes are thirsty for HIM.

What else may be the height of sorrow expressed by Surdas in the song!

Similar pangs of love and devotion towards the Lord Krishna, Meerabai (of 16th Century) had expressed in her *kirtanas* (*bhajans*). As we all know, she dedicated her life to Lord Krishna, composed songs of deep devotion, and she was one of the poet-saints of the *Bhakti* movement. The characteristic of her poetry is a complete surrender to her Lord and the spiritual joy and ecstasy she felt of union with HIM through her *bhajans*. In the following *bhajan* / song, Meerabai considered Sri Krishna to be her beloved Husband and expresses her love for HIM as she submerged herself into a reverie or deep contemplation of separation from her deity and the ensuing despondency.

हे री मैं तो प्रेमदिवानी मेरो दरद न जाणै कोय
दरद की मारी बन बन डोलूं बैद मिल्यो नही
कोई॥

घायल की गति घायल जाणै, जो कोई घायल होय
जौहरि की गति जौहरी जाणै की जिन जौहर
होय ॥
हे री मैं तो प्रेमदिवानी मेरो दरद न जाणै कोय

सूली ऊपर सेज हमारी, सोवण किस बिध होय
गगन मंडल पर सेज पिया की, मिलणा किस
बिध होय ॥
हे री मैं तो प्रेमदिवानी मेरो दरद न जाणै कोय

दरद की मारी बनबन डोलूं बैद मिल्या नहिं
कोय
मीरा की प्रभु पीर मिटेगी जद बैद सांवरिया
होय ॥

Meerabai

The song starts with Meerabai crying aloud, *"main to prem divani -* meaning that:

" I am madly in love with Krishna!"

and meaning of the song is:

O my friend! I have become mad in love for Krishna. No one knows my pain.

Only the wounded knows the agony of the wounded. Only jewellers can value jewels.

My bed is on pins and needles and how can I sleep? My Lord's bed is in the Heavens. How can I meet HIM?

Hit by pain I wander from jungle to jungle. There is no doctor to cure me.

Only when My Lord becomes doctor, I secure healing.

Further notes: Meera's SONGS are the most beautiful ever sung by any devotee…

Perhaps this song gives us a good understanding of her deep devotion and her complete feeling of surrender to her Lord. She was a princess, a queen, but she renounced the palace to be a beggar on the streets. Playing her veena and dancing in ecstasy, she marched from village to village, town to town, city to city, singing her heart out, pouring herself out totally in devotion towards Krishna.

One finds in Meerabai's devotional songs, a philosophical connotation or undertone that describes her profound love and deep hearty salutation to the Lord Sri Krishna. All prayers of these profound devotees are indeed soul-touching entreaties for HIS grace and they are indicators of their unmistakable and obvious earnestness to reach *Paramaatma*. How much solid resolve and firm conviction they had exhibited in their worship against all odds in their lives! Singing is the most sublime way of worship to the God almighty residing in this temple of this body.

If we again remind ourselves with the *ashtapadis* in Gita Govindam of the poet Jayadeva, one finds them to be a candid or sincere depiction or portrayal of misery or agony felt by a devotee separated from her / his Lord. The following particular *ashtapadi* is a poignant and soul-touching way of expressing love coupled with sincere devotion as well as deep distress of a devotee!

निन्दति चन्दनमिन्दुकिरणमनु विन्दति खेदमधीरम् ।

व्यालनिलयमिलनेन गरलमिव कलयति मलयसमीरम् ॥

माधव मनसिजविशिखभयादिव भावनया त्वयि लीना

सा विरहे तव दीना ॥ १॥

अविरलनिपतितमदनशरादिव भवदवनाय विशालम् ।

स्वहृदयमर्मणि वर्म करोति सजलनलिनीदलजालम् ॥ २॥

सा विरहे तव दीना

प्रतिपदमिदमपि निगदति माधव तव चरणे पतिताहम् ।

त्वयि विमुखे मयि सपदि सुधानिधिरपि तनुते तनुदाहम् ॥ ६॥

सा विरहे तव दीना

ध्यानलयेन पुरः परिकल्प्य भवन्तमतीव दुरापम् ।

विलपति हसति विषीदति रोदिति चञ्चति मुञ्चति तापम् ॥ ७॥

सा विरहे तव दीना

Jayadeva

Meaning: The song starts with a description of the sorrowful state of Radha due to the separation from Krishna.

Radha scorns or dislikes everything. She treats even the scent of sandalwood paste as a poison. She is not able to derive any peace from all the surroundings. She is stricken by grief and is fully immersed / absorbed in Krishna's thoughts only.

The love-God Manmadha is continuously shooting flowery arrows at Radha's heart. But she is not caring for this and she is busy preparing a lotus-petal shield to protect the Lord instead. She imagines that she has concealed HIM in her heart and she desires that the lotus petals guards HIM from the arrows.

Radha remembers HIM only on each step of hers. Because she imagines that HE is not caring for her and the moon who is supposed to be very comforting, is also causing her lot of grief.

HE fills her mind. Radha always think of HIM only. She fully meditates on HIM. She thinks that HE is in her front, Sometimes she laughs, sometimes she weeps, wanders here and there, and behaves like a lady in mental sickness.

Gita Govindam has been a perfect inspiration for many musical compositions. Here, I also wish to remember a *sloka* in *Sivamanasapuja* of Adi Sankaracharya. It projects the most expressive and animated way of a prayer to *Paramaatma* by a devotee seeking for HIS compassion. The *sloka* follows:

आत्मा त्वं गिरिजा मतिः सहचराः प्राणाः शरीरं गृहं

पूजा ते विषयोपभोगरचना निद्रा समाधिस्थितिः ।

सञ्चारः पदयोः प्रदक्षिणविधिः स्तोत्राणि सर्वा गिरो

यद्यत्कर्म करोमि तत्तदखिलं शम्भो तवाराधनम् ॥४॥

Sivamanasapuja

Adi Sankaracharya

<u>Meaning:</u> O *Paramaatma*, YOU are my *aatma* (soul), Devi Girija, the Divine Mother is my *buddhi* (intellect), YOUR companions are my *prana* (vital airs), my body is YOUR temple, my interactions with this mortal world are YOUR worship and my sleep is *samaadhi* (absorption in YOU), my walk is YOUR *Pradakshina* (circumambulation), all my speech is YOUR praise, Oh! Sambho! whatever work I do is YOUR *aradhana* (Worship).

This is all *maanasica puja* (mental worship) which a true devotee makes (within her/his mind) to *Paramaatma* as amply made clear to us by Jayadeva, Meerabai or Surdas or all other devotees by their songs/ *bhajans*. *Paramaatma is aatma* residing in a body and this fact one needs to recognize as pronounced by Bhagawaan Sri Krishna in the following *sloka* in *Kshetra Kshetrajna Yoga*:

उपद्रष्टानुमन्ता च भर्ता भोक्ता महेश्वरः ।

परमात्मेति चाप्युक्तो देहेऽस्मिन्पुरुषः परः ॥ २२ ॥

Kshetra Kshetrajna Yoga

> **Meaning:** The *aatma* or soul in this body is *Paramaatma*; HE is the witness, i.e. the overseer, the approver, the *bharta* (supporter) and the Supreme Self.

Bhagawaan's mercy is infinite and HE is magnanimous in forgiving all follies that a person like me might commit in ignorance. A devotee with *ananya bhakti* is sure to get the strength needed to overcome all mundane sufferings and also receive HIS benevolence and grace to reach HIS abode of everlasting joy. With this conviction, let us proceed to the next chapter *"Bhakti and Bliss"*.

CHAPTER 4

Bhakti and Bliss

Krishna and gopikas in rasa kreeda - Adharam madhuram

Before I proceed into the chapter, I wish to recollect the most pleasant and delightful devotional song *"Adharam madhuram…"* in *Madhurashtakam,* a devotional composition written in Sanskrit by the poet Vallabhacharya[27] (15th century). He is a saint and philosopher who originally belongs to Andhra region in South India and who has established his philosophy of *Pushti Marga, (i.e.,* the Path of Grace) in North India according to which a devotee sees only Sri Krishna and none other than Lord Krishna everywhere. The word 'Ashtakam' is derived from the Sanskrit word *aṣṭa,* meaning "eight".

---

27 Vallabhacharya was a saint and philosopher. He was one of the important exponents of the devotional bhakti movement. He founded the Kṛiṣhṇa-centered *Puṣṭi Mārga* and expounded the philosophy of *Suddhadvaita* – purely non-dual philosophy focusing on the worship of the deity Krishna only. Vallabhacharya rejected asceticism and hermitic life, preaching that any householder can achieve salvation through *ananya bhakti* towards Sri Krishna,. He authored many texts – a commentary on the *Brahma Sutras, Shodasa Grantha* and several commentaries on the *Bhāgavata Purāṇa*

अधरं मधुरं वदनं मधुरं
नयनं मधुरं हसितं मधुरम् ।
हृदयं मधुरं गमनं मधुरं
मधुराधिपतेरखिलं मधुरम् ॥ 1 ॥
वचनं मधुरं चरितं मधुरं
वसनं मधुरं वलितं मधुरं ।
चलितं मधुरं भ्रमितं मधुरं
मधुराधिपतेरखिलं मधुरम् ॥ 2 ॥
वेणु-मधुरो रेणु-मधुरः
पाणि-मधुरः पादौ मधुरौ ।
नृत्यं मधुरं सख्यं मधुरं
मधुराधिपतेरखिलं मधुरम् ॥ 3 ॥

Vallabhacharya

<u>Meaning</u>: In the song, the devotee sings as if the Lord is before him. As if in a trance, he is attracted by the beauty of Bhagawaan Sri Krishna in everything that belongs to the Lord – the beautiful face, the beautiful lips, the beautiful eyes, the beautiful smile, the Lord's beautiful stride. For the devotee, even the Lord's *murali* or flute is beautiful, the lord's hands and the Lord's legs are beautiful and Lord's every *anuvu* or every atom is beautiful in the devotee's mind.

<u>Further notes:</u> *Madhurashtakam* contains just eight hymns, i.e., eight stanzas only. *Madhurashtakam*, as the name itself indicates, is filled with '*madhuryam*' or sweetness. There is no other composition in Sanskrit which is so enchanting and soul-soothing as *Madhurashtakam*. The composition is a pinnacle of *bhakti* towards *Paramaatma*. All the eight verses are brimming or filled with full of love and devotion to Krishna in the form of a transcendental or divine singing by a devotee

Bhakti and Bliss

What *Bhakti* cannot do! This remark, as enunciated by Adi Sankaracharya in *Sivanadalahari* and as we understood in the introduction of this book, must permeate or flood our minds in every moment of this mortal life. We have ample knowledge on this aspect from the lives of many devotees who immersed themselves in HIS prayers and incessant worship and who constantly engaged in singing in HIS tribute even while they had been going through the most critical moments in their lives. In fact, this must clear our doubt - lingering in our tiny and immature minds particularly more in times of our troubles and difficulties - about HIS presence, manifestations and HIS all-pervading effervescence in this mortal world. Even mere reminiscence or remembrance of HIS divine manifestations and graceful acts that bestowed salvation to these devotees must fill into every cell and fiber of our being.

All these great devotees adopted *bhakti yoga* as a path to self-realization and salvation. It is also true that they are *karma yogis* denouncing all the worldly attachments and perceiving *Paramaatma* in every being and immersing themselves *manasa, vaacha* and *karmana* in HIS praise through their *bhajans* and songs. They tasted the nectar of HIS bliss every moment of their life. Here, we need to remind ourselves of Bhagawaan's sacred message in Bhagavad Gita given on many occasions:

बाह्यस्पर्शेष्वसक्तात्मा विन्दत्यात्मनि यत्सुखम् ।

स ब्रह्मयोगयुक्तात्मा सुखमक्षयमश्नुते ॥ २१॥

Karmasanyasa yoga

Meaning: With the mind unattached to external contacts, HIS devotee discovers happiness in the self and engaged wholeheartedly in the meditation of *Paramaatma* he attains eternal bliss.

प्रशान्तमनसं होनं योगिनं सुखमुत्तमम् ।
उपैति शान्तरजसं ब्रह्मभूतमकल्मषम् ॥ २७ ॥

Aatmasayama yoga

Meaning: For the yogi whose mind is wholly composed and whose passions are assuaged or soothed, Supreme bliss comes and he is free from sin and becomes one with *Paramaatma.*

मां च योऽव्यभिचारेण भक्तियोगेन सेवते ।
स गुणान्समतीत्यैतान्ब्रह्मभूयाय कल्पते ॥ २६ ॥

Gunatriyavibhaga yoga

Meaning: The devotee who serves HIM with *ananya bhakti* and is beyond the three *gunas*[28], is eligible for attaining the absolute bliss.

सर्वकर्माण्यपि सदा कुर्वाणो मद्व्यपाश्रयः ।
मत्प्रसादादवाप्नोति शाश्वतं पदमव्ययम् ॥ ५६।

Mokshasanyasa yoga

Meaning: Those, who always take refuge in HIM, obtain by HIS grace the eternal, indestructible state or abode even while doing all actions in the mortal life

As we can comprehend from the lives of all the devotees, ananya bhkti which is pure or untainted by self-interest and unshakeable faith leads anyone to a state which is unbearable to forget *Paramaatma* even for a moment. It is only by God's grace, one attains that eminence of *ananya bhakti.* Once attained, he considers the mind, intellect, the body and the

---

28 Each being in this birth is typified by the presence of the three *gunas - sattva, rajas and tamas* and the resulting *vikaaraas* (like anger, desire, happiness, grief), that engulf him by *maya* (delusion) prevent him to perceive *Paramaatma*, the *Nirguna* and the Eternal Self.

organs as belonging to *Paramaatma*, treats himself as a means in HIS hand and always dwells in reciting HIS names and singing HIS glory and grandeur.

It is illuminating to hear to the melodious *bhajanas* (songs) of Sant Kabirdas[29] (of 15th century) who promoted the path of *bhakti* and *renunciation* to realize the Supreme *Paramaatma* and derive the limitless and abundant bliss through constant prayers on HIM. In one *bhajan*, Kabir advises: "You don't need to go to the temple to worship. Just close your eyes and think of the almighty in your heart. You don't need to go for pilgrimage. Just think of Ganga and Yamuna in your heart and take a dip in water (by *maanasica puja*). Pure intention and meditation are the key to achieve anything in life". The following *bhajan* remarkably displays his conviction and faith in *Paramaatma* and celebrates the joy of poverty, and the beauty of simplicity. The joy of remembering and meditating on HIM is far greater than the joy afforded by material comfort or luxury, Kabir says in the song.

मन लागो मेरो यार फकीरी में। जो सुख पावो राम भजन में, सो सुख नाही अमीरी में ॥ भला बुरा सब का सुन लीजै, कर गुजरान गरीबी में ॥ प्रे	

---

29 Kabir was born in the city of Varanasi, Uttar Pradesh, India. Kabir was a disciple of Swami Ramananda, the poet-saint of his times. Kabir was known for his strong conviction towards Advaita philosophy teaching that All-pervading God resides in all objects – animate or inanimate. He was known for being critical of rituals and dogmatic practices plaguing the minds of the mankind. His writings had influenced Bhakti movement and his verses are found in Guru Granth Sahib. His legacy continues through the Kabir *panth* - Path of Kabir.

म नगर में रहिनी हमारी,

भली बन आई सबुरी में ॥

हाथ में खूंडी, बगल में सोटा,

चारो दिशा जागीरी में ॥

आखिर यह तन ख़ाक मिलेगा,

कहाँ फिरत मगरूरी में ॥

कहत कबीर सुनो भाई साधो,

साहिब मिले सबुरी में ।

Sant Kabir

Meaning:

Oh friend, my mind enjoys living free like a fakir!

I don't get that joy in riches and luxury.

I rejoice in poverty. My mind rejoices in simplicity.

I carry only a bowl and a stick and yet my kingdom lies in all directions.

I live in the city of love and contentment.

This body will finally merge with the earth one day. Why to be so arrogant?

Says Kabir, listen friends, you find the Lord in your patience.

Whatever we hear from these great devotees is the absolute truth and it is the very truth we have received from Bhagawaan Sri Krishna in Bhagavad Gita. Kabir was a strong advocator of 'nirguna puja' and in this context, he also expressed his conviction that realizing *Nirguna Paramaatma* is not easy, but a single-minded devotion and dedication only help to realize HIM and the result is brightness, eternal peace and comfort. Sant Kabir says that one is fortunate to be born as human being with a body that must be considered as a precious gift and it is important to make good use of this gift, to wear it with great care and to return it back as good as was received. How much mind-searching and truthful it is!

Like Narayaneeyam which is written in a style easy, even for ignorant persons like me to understand the abstruse or complex concepts of philosophy and to deepen their faith in the plain theme of *bhakti* and its practice, we get greatly illuminated by *Sri Krishna Karnamritam* of Leela Suka[30] (of 13th century). Because he was so engrossed in visualization of *leela* (the divine acts) of Sri Krishna and because he filled *SriKrishna Karnamritam* with detailed and beautiful description of this divine *leela* like Sukamaharshi[31], he was fondly known as Leela suka. *Amrita* means nectar. *Karnamrita* means nectar to ears implying that it is nectar to those who hear about Lord Sri Krishna. The following *sloka* abundantly brings forth the poet's deep devotion towards *Paramaatma* and his adoration and love in dripping himself in HIS thoughts and memories:

---

30 The original name of Leela Suka is Bilvamangala. He was born in Kerala, India and lived in the 13th century. According to legend, Bilvamangala concentrated all of his time and attention on a courtesan called Cintamani. Cintamani advised Bilvamangala that had he diverted even one thousandth part of his love on her towards the Lord Krishna, he would attain eternal joy, This, by the divine grace of the Lord, transformed his life in a moment and he became a great devotee for which she is hailed as his guru in the composition. Bilvamangala travelled to Brindavan, where he spent his final days and worked on the composition of *SriKrishna Karnamritam*. His pleasant Sanskrit mingled with the ecstatic love towards Krishna filled his songs with a quality so rare that when sung they are nectar to the ears (*Karnamritam*).

31 Sukamaharshi is the son of the sage Veda Vyasa. He is enriched with supreme knowledge by birth. As he has the ability of repeating everything whatever he has heard, he is known by the name 'suka' (meaning 'parrot'). Sukamaharshi surpassed his father in spiritual attainment. Once, when following his son, Veda Vyasa encountered a group of celestial fairies who were bathing. Sukamaharshi's purity was so great that the fairies did not consider him to be a distraction, even though they were naked. But they covered themselves when they encountered his father Veda Vyasa. It is Sukamaharshi who described *Bhagavata Purana* to the king Parikshit when the latter was destined to die after seven days due to a curse.

भक्तिस्त्वयि स्थिरतरा भगवन् यदि स्या-
दैवेन नः फलितदिव्यकिशोरवेषे ।
मुक्तिः स्वयं मुकुलिताञ्जलि सेवतेऽस्मान्
धर्मार्थकामगतयः समयप्रतीक्षाः ॥ १.१०७॥

SriKrishna Karnamritam

Leelasuka

Meaning: To our good fortune, YOU appeared before us in YOUR child form. If our devotion towards YOU is firm, then salvation will come to us of its own accord with folded hands. The other three *purusharthaas*[32] - *dharma, artha* and *kama* - will automatically wait their turn to serve us.

The poet implies in the above *sloka* that devotees who do not want anything else except to sing of Him, think of Him and love Him, shun (or spurn or reject) all *purusharthaas* and moksha (salvation) even. For them, the bliss of *bhakthi* is enough. Every *sloka* in *SriKrishna Karnamritam* bountifully carries the poet's intense fervor and boundless devotion (*ananya bhakti*) towards Bhagawaan Sri Krishna. One more beautiful composition of Leelasuka in admiration to Krishna is contained in the following *sloka*:

---

32 *Purusharthas* mean the four objectives of a human life, namely *dharma* (righteousness), *artha* (prosperity), *kama* (desire) and *moksha* (liberation / self-realization)

> ## जय जय जय देव देव देव त्रिभुवनमङ्गलदिव्यनामधेय ।
> जय जय जय बालकृष्णदेव श्रवणमनोनयनामृतावतार ॥ १.१०८ ॥
>
> *SriKrishna Karnamritam*
>
> **Meaning:** Salutations to YOU, Oh Lord of all deities!. Oh Krishna! YOUR name purifies all the three worlds. As a child, YOU are the nectar of ears, eyes and mind, i.e., *sravanamrita*, nectar to those who hear about HIM, *manomrita,* nectar to the mind of those who think about HIM *and nayanamrita*, nectar to those who see HIS form.

Sri Rama is *Paramaatma*'s incarnation in *Treta yuga* as Sri Krishna in *Dwapur yuga.* These incarnations, as clarified by Bhagawaan Sri Krishna HIMSELF in Bhagavad Gita, are displayed in this mortal world in physical form whenever there was a decline of *dharma* (righteousness) and rise of *adharma* (unrighteousness), and so are meant to protect the virtuous and to destroy the wicked and to establish righteousness in this mortal world. The following song by Sadasiva Brahmendra on Sri Rama is so enchanting and thought provoking that it embraces the whole purport of Bhagavad Gita.

పిబరే రామరసం పిబరే రామరసం

పిబరే రామరసం రసనే పిబరే
రామరసం...

పిబరే రామరసం రసనే పిబరే
రామరసం;

రామరసం

జనన మరణ భయ శోకవిదూరం

జనన మరణ భయ శోకవిదూరం
సకల శాస్త్ర

నిగమాగమ సారం

జనన మరణ భయ శోకవిదూరం
సకల శాస్త్ర

నిగమాగమ సారం

పిబరే రామరసం పిబరే రామరసం

పిబరే రామరసం రసనే పిబరే
రామరసం

పిబరే రామరసం రసనో ఫిబరే
రామరసం

రామరసం

శుద్ధ పరమహంస ఆశ్రమ గీతం

శుద్ధ పరమహంస ఆశ్రమ గీతం సుఖ
శానక

కౌశిక ముఖ పీఠం

శుద్ధ పరమహంస ఆశ్రమ గీతం సుఖ
శానక

Sadasiva Brahmendra

కాశిక ముఖ పీఠం పిబరే రామరసం రసనే పిబరే రామరసం పిబరే రామరసం రసనే పిబరే రామరసం రామరసం రామరసం రామరసం	
'Rasane, Pibare Rama rasam' means - Oh| Tongue, drink the essence in the name of Sri Rama. In the lyrics of this soul-touching song, we find the following meaning: — By drinking the essence in the name of Sri Rama, it will help you remove your sins, — It will help you to be far removed from the grief or sorrow of the cycle of birth and death — It is the essence of all the Sastras *i.e.,* holy treatises *i.e.,* the Vedas and Sciences. — It will purify even the most impious or impure person — It is the purest song under which Paramahamsa (pure devotees like the poet) has taken refuge or taken shelter — It is the same nectar-like drink taken by sages like Suka, Saunaka and Kaushika.	

Purandaradasa[33] (- a philosopher of 15th Century). deriving his inspiration from the three features of musical traditions of Karnataka,

---

33 Puranadaradasa adopted *sanyasa* (renunciation of worldly relations) since his childhood and is a composer and singer. He was one of the chief founding proponents of Carnatic music. He is a devotional singer who made the difficult Sanskrit tenets of *Bhagavata Purana* available to everyone in simple and melodious songs. His compositions are mostly in Kannada language and some are in Sanskrit.

Maharashtra and Hindusthani, composed many *krithis* or *kirtanas* and songs each of which is replete or filled with his absolute devotional fervor. He followed the footsteps of the great Annamacharya. He is an ardent devotee of Lord Venkateswara of Tirumala (popularly known as TTD in Andhra Pradesh). One popular *krithi* written in Kannada language in reverence to the Lord is:

ವೆಂಕಟಾಚಲ ನಿಲಯಂ, ವೈಕುಂಠ ಪುರ ವಾಸಂ

ಪಂಕಜನೇತ್ರಂ ಪರಮಪವಿತ್ರಂ

ಶಂಖ ಚಕ್ರಧರಂ ಚಿನ್ಮಯ ರೂಪಂ

||ವೆಂಕಟಾಚಲ||

ಅಂಬುಜೋದ್ಭವ ವಿನುತಂ

ಅಗಣಿತಗುಣ ನಾಮಂ||ಅಂಬು||

ತುಂಬುರು ನಾರದ ಗಾನ ವಿಲೋಲಂ

ಅಂಬುದಿಶಯನಂ ಆತ್ಮಾಭಿರಾಮಂ

||ವೆಂಕಟಾಚಲ||

ಪಾಹಿ ಪಾಂಡವ ಪಕ್ಷಂ, ಕೌರವ ಮದಹರಣಂ

ಬಾಹು ಪರಾಕ್ರಮ ಪೂರ್ಣಂ

ಅಹಲ್ಯಾ ಶಾಪಭಯ ನಿವಾರಣಂ

||ವೆಂಕಟಾಚಲ|||

ಸಕಲವೇದ ವಿಚಾರಂ, ಸರ್ವ ಜೀವನಿಕರಂ

ಮಕರ ಕುಂಡಲಧರ, ಮದನ ಗೋಪಾಲಂ

ಭಕ್ತ ಪೋಷಕ ಶ್ರೀ ಪುರಂದರ ವಿಠಲಂ

||ವೆಂಕಟಾಚಲ||

Purandaradasa

This song is about Venkatachala (known as Tirumala in Andhra Pradesh, India), which is believed to be the abode of Lord Vishnu, who dwells there as Lord Venkateswara.

Meaning of the *kirtana*: HE is the residing deity on Venkata mountain and lives in Vaikunta,

HE has lotus like eyes. HE is divinely pure and has divine form carrying the conch and the discus and HIS form is full of pure consciousness.

HE is worshipped by Brahma and has innumerable names and characters,

HE relishes music by Narada and Thumbura *rishis* (sages).

HE is Gopala, the God of love and wears golden ear studs. HE is the protector of his devotees and is always present to help them in their spiritual journey.

HE is also known as the Lord of Purandara who is a great devotee of Lord Vishnu.

Another familiar and revered name to Lord Venkateswara is Govinda and the following song by Purandaradasa is a prayer addressing the Lord by this name Govinda and offering himself at the feet of the Lord.

ಗೋವಿಂದ ನಿನ್ನ ನಾಮವೆ ಚೆಂದ

ಅಣುರೇಣು ತೃಣಕಾಷ್ಟ ಪರಿಪೂರ್ಣ ಗೋವಿಂದ

ನಿರ್ಮಲಾತ್ಮಕನಾಗಿ ಇರುವುದೇ ಆನಂದ

ಗೋವಿಂದ ಗೋವಿಂದ ನಿನ್ನ ನಾಮವೆ ಚೆಂದ

ಸೃಷ್ಟಿ ಸ್ಥಿತಿ ಲಯ ಕಾರಣ ಗೋವಿಂದ

ಈ ಪರಿ ಮಹಿಮೆಯ ತಿಳಿಯುವುದಾನಂದ

ಗೋವಿಂದ ನಿನ್ನ ನಾಮವೆ ಚೆಂದ

ಪರಮಪುರುಷ ಶ್ರೀ ಪುರಂದರ ವಿಠಲನ

ಹಿಂಗದ ದಾಸರ ನೆನೆಯುವುದಾನಂದ

ಗೋವಿಂದ ಗೋವಿಂದ ನಿನ್ನ ನಾಮವೆ ಚೆಂದ

Song of Purandaradasa

<u>Meaning:</u>

Oh Govinda! YOUR name itself is a beauty.

Oh Govinda! the one present in all beings, starting from the micro atoms, dust particles, blades of grass to dry branches and everything in this universe, knowing this reality and living with clear conscience about YOU is a great joy.

Oh Govinda! the one responsible for the creation, protection and destruction of the universe and its beings, knowing this truth itself about YOU is a great joy.

Oh *Parama Purusha*[34]!, Purandara Vithala[35]!, moving with you in servitude is itself a great joy.

---

34   the most acclaimed one
35   deity in Pandaripura, Gujarat, India

In the above scintillating song, Purandaradasa addresses the Lord as the *antharyaami* (in-dweller) residing inside the crores and crores of *chetanas* (animate beings) and *achetanas* (inanimate beings) of HIS universe.

Here, I remind myself of one more song in the name of Govinda sung by Annamaya, the well-known composer as well as a singer in praise of Lord Venkateswara.

గోవింద గోవిందయని కొలువరే
గోవిందాయని కొలువరే
హరియచ్యుతాయని పాడరే
పురుషోత్తమాయని పొగడరే
పరమపురుషాయని పలుకరే
సిరివరయనుచును చెలగరే జనులు
గోవింద గోవిందా యని కొలువరే

పాండవవరదా అని పాడరే
అండజవాహను కొనియాడరే
కొండలరాయనినే కోరరే
దండితో మాధవునినే తలచరో జనులు
గోవింద గోవిందా యని కొలువరే
దేవుడు శ్రీవిభుడని తెలియరే
శోభలయనంతుని చూడరే
శ్రీవేంకటనాథుని చేరరే
పావనమైయొప్పుడును బతుకరే జనులు
గోవింద గోవిందా యని కొలువరే

Annamaya

Meaning: Annamaya addressing all people, he exhorts them and vehemently asks them

- to sing in the name of *Paramaatma* as Govinda,
- to dance in ecstasy reciting the names of *Achyuta* and Hari, *i.e.,* Sri Maha Vishnu,

- to praise HIM as *Purushottama*, the supreme being,
- to praise HIM as embodiment of prosperity.
- He asks the people:
- to praise HIM as the benefactor of Pandavas,
- to sing in Praise of *Paramaatm*a who sits on the celestial Garuda *vahana* (chariot).

He says: People should enjoy the splendor of the eternal *Ananta, i.e.,*

Paramaatma and surrender to Lord Venkatanadha, *i.e.* Lord Venkateswara.

Why don't the people live piously?

Everything has to end finally. Here, I am destined to pen my closing words to this book in the form of salutations to *Paramaatma* by reminiscing the following poem in MahaBhagavatamu of the poet Potana.

Sri Krishna, the Bestower of Liberation / Self-realization

శ్రీకృష్ణా! యదుభూషణా! నరసఖా! శృంగారరత్నాకరా!

లోక్రదోహి న్రరేంద్రవంశదహనా! లోకేశ్వరా! దేవతా

నీ్రబాహ్మణగోగణార్తిహరణా! నిర్వాణసంధాయకా!

నీకున్ ్రమొక్కెద్రం దుంపవే భవలతల్ నిత్యానుకంపానిధీ!

Meaning: Oh! Sri Krishna! Friend of Arjuna! Jewel of *Yadu vamsa* (Yadu dynasty)! Destroyer of wicked rulers in this world! Eternal ruler of this universe! Saviour and provider of happiness to all beings (including all divine deities and cows) in distress, Bestower of *moksha* (liberation / self-realization)! I offer my earnest prayers to YOU. Oh! King of compassion! I request you to liberate me from this mundane worldly shackles.

The Epilogue

Bhagawaan Sri Krishna, The Viswa Guru

This life has in addition to any other goal - more importantly - a spiritual goal. One needs to recognize this, nay, it awaits to be recognized by most of the ignorant souls like me. For this, the foremost ingredient is to develop an appreciating eye for the beings and objects around and in short for the mysterious creator of this world where she, he, you, and I are born and are living together. Once the revelation that HE is omnipresent and all-pervading dawns on us, we need to reinforce it with self-enquiry or self-introspection. Then, *ananya bhakti* towards HIM sprouts in us. It gently overtakes and cleans the mind of evil propensities or tendencies like desire, anger and greed which Bhagwaan Sri Krishna castigated in *Daivaasura Sampad Vibhhaaga Yoga* as the most destructive features in a human's life:

त्रिविधं नरकस्येदं द्वारं नाशनमात्मनः ।
कामः क्रोधस्तथा लोभस्तस्मादेतत्त्रयं त्यजेत् ॥ २१ ॥

Daivaasura Sampad Vibhhaaga Yoga

Meaning: One must abandon the triple hellish qualities – lust, anger and greed – which are destructive of the Self

---

Thus, with '*aatmavinigrahah*', *i.e.*, with restlessness removed and mind getting steady and fully disciplined, devotion towards *Paramaatma* provides the necessary strength and forbearance to remain unshaken under all circumstances of obstacles and hardships. This has been amply revealed from the lives of all the Godly personalities whom we are aware of and whom we have tried here to remember through their songs. These blessed devotees / souls continued throughout their lives to meditate and devote on *Paramaatma* in their own way of pure *worship* without expecting anything in return. Their lives are glorious indicator of *ananya bhakti* leading to *saranagti* or total surrender to their beloved God and also many a time leading to unbearable pain or *agony* whenever not able to bear separation from HIM and thirsting for an union with HIM and finally becoming dear to Him and enjoying the eternal *bliss*.

With my meagre familiarity and knowledge limited to only a few devotees of our times, I tried in this book to highlight their devotional songs to the best of my ability. I may be excused for any faulty expression within this my tiny attempt. Nevertheless, I bow in reverence to *Paramaatma* in bestowing this opportunity of deriving immense pleasure through these songs and of enriching myself with Supreme knowledge embedded therein.

In conclusion, with the devotional songs of all these devotees still lingering in my mind, I further wish to remind myself with the sublime message given by Bhagawaan Sri Krishna in *Mokshasanyasa yoga* along with the simple truth about the required mode of life to be practiced as a human being.

बुद्ध्या विशुद्ध्या युक्तो धृत्यात्मानं नियम्य च।

शब्दादीन्विषयांस्त्यक्त्वा रागद्वेषौ व्युदस्य च ॥५१॥

विविक्तसेवी लघ्वाशी यतवाक्कायमानसः ।

ध्यानयोगपरो नित्यं वैराग्यं समुपाश्रितः ॥ ५२ ॥

अहङ्कारं बलं दर्प कामं क्रोधं परिग्रहम् ।

विमुच्य निर्ममः शान्तो ब्रह्मभूयाय कल्पते ॥ ५३ ॥

Mokshasanyasa Yoga

Meaning: Whoever restrains himself with pure intellect, keeps away from sense objects and also from feelings of both hatred and attraction, dwells in solitude, eats little, subdues his speech, body and mind, engages himself in meditation and concentration, forsakes egoism, arrogance, desire, anger and is free of possessiveness and maintains tranquillity in mind, he becomes worthy of becoming dear and near to *Paramaatma*.

In the above *slokas*, *Paramaatma* as *Viswaguru* (Divine teacher) in the incarnation of Bhagawaan Sri Krishna showed HIS benevolence in presenting succinctly or concisely the steps for *saadhana* or practice of *karma yoga* and to be finally worthy of earning HIS grace. I pray HIM to give me, a commoner amongst multitude of commoners in this world, the strength to sincerely and faithfully follow HIS advice.

Om Namo Bhagavate Vasudevaya   ***Om Namah Sivaya***

Om tat sat

I Salute My Loving Deity Anjaneya

मनोजवं मारुततुल्यवेगं

जितेन्द्रियं बुद्धिमतां वरिष्ठ ।

वातात्मजं वानरयूथमुख्यं श्री

रामदूतं शरणं प्रपद्ये ।

Meaning of the verse:

I salute my ideal deity Anjaneya who is swift as the mind and fast as the wind, who is the master of the senses, who is known for his exceptional intelligence, learning and wisdom and who is the son of the wind God and chief among the _vanaras_[36]. From that messenger of Sri Rama, the God incarnate, I seek for refuge by prostrating before him.

---

36 Forest dwelling people depicted in the epic _Ramayana_ (of _Treta yuga_) as having the characteristics of monkeys; Described to be possessing supernatural abilities and purported to be created to help _Sri Rama_ (God incarnate) in defeating the _asura_ (demon) king _Ravana_.